HIGH SCHOOL ENGL
PRACTICAL LANGUAGE

- WHAT YOU NEED TO KNOW AS YOU PROGRESS ON A HIGH SCHOOL LEVEL

HIGH SCHOOL ENGLISH LEVEL 3

THE SKILLS AND TOOLS NEEDED TO BE CONFIDENT AT HIGH SCHOOL LEVEL

BY

PAUL MEADE

MEDIA LITERACY CONSULTING

LEARN ENGLISH WHILE YOU PLAY

AS YOU CONTINUE YOUR LEARNING JOURNEY, WE TRUST YOU HAVE ALREADY GONE THROUGH THE LEVEL 2 BOOK WITH EASE. ALTHOUGH MANY OF THE FUNDAMENTAL ELEMENTS ARE THE SAME IN THIS BOOK, THE TASKS ARE HARDER, MORE ADVANCED, AND REQUIRE A BIT MORE EFFORT.

WE ALSO INTRODUCE NEW CONCEPTS - VITAL TO YOUR DEVELOPMENT OF ENGLISH LANGUAGE SKILLS.

Published by Media Literacy Consulting, UK

www.medialiteracyconsulting.com

THE MENU OF FUN

Full Stop or Period (•) - is used to indicate the end of a sentence or a statement. It is also used in abbreviations. Example: "I went to the shops."

Comma (,) - is used to separate items in a list, provide pauses in a sentence, or separate clauses. Example: "I need to buy apples, oranges, and bananas."

Question mark (?) - is used at the end of a sentence to indicate a direct question. Example: "What time is the meeting?"

Exclamation mark (!) - is used to indicate strong emotions, surprise, or emphasis.
Example: "That's amazing!"

Quotation marks (" ") - are used to enclose direct speech, diaogue, or a quote from someone. Example: She said, "Hello, how are you?"

Colon (:) - is used to introduce a list, an explanation, or a quotation. Example: "I have three favorite colors: blue, green, and purple."

Semicolon (;) - is used to connect two closely related independent clauses or to separate items in a list when those items already contain commas. Example: "I have to finish my work; then I can go home."

Dash (—) - is used to indicate a break or interruption in a sentence or to emphasize a particular point. Example: "She loved two things—traveling and reading."

Parentheses or brackets ( ) - are used to enclose additional information or explanations that are not crucial to the main sentence. Example: "The event (which was held outdoors) was a great success."

Ellipsis (• • •) - is used to indicate the omission of words, a pause, or trailing off in thought. Example: "I don't know... it's just..."

Hyphen (-) - is used to join words together or to indicate a word break at the end of a line. Example: "Well-being" or "twenty-one."

Apostrophe (') - is used to **indicate possession** or to **form contractions**. Example: "John's car" or "can't" (instead of "cannot"). If a single person or thing owns something, the apostrophe comes before the 'S. If more than one person owns something, the apostrophe comes after the S'. - The Boy's book (single boy), The boys' books (several boys).

Level 2 punctuation

1. what do you use before but and because

   A ☐ apostrophe B ☐ full stop

   C ☐ comma D ☐ question mark

2. when do you use a apostrophe

   A ☐ ending a sentence

   B ☐ replacing a conjunction

   C ☐ sentence starters

   D ☐ replacing a letter don't can't

3. what do you use a semicolon for

   A ☐ replacing a conjunction

   B ☐ starting a list

   C ☐ starting or ending speech

   D ☐ separating a sentence

4. what do you put when you start a list

   A ☐ apostrophe B ☐ colon

   C ☐ semicolon D ☐ comma

5. what do you use a question mark for

   A ☐ being angry at someone

   B ☐ asking a question

   C ☐ replacing a conjunction

   D ☐ starting a list

6. when do you a exclamation mark

   A ☐ separating a sentence

   B ☐ ending a sentence

   C ☐ when are yelling at someone

   D ☐ replacing a conjunction

7. what do you put at the end of a sentence

   A ☐ comma B ☐ semicolon

   C ☐ question mark D ☐ full stop

8. what do you sometimes use at a end of a paragraph

   A ☐ ellipsis B ☐ exclamation mark

   C ☐ apostrophe D ☐ colon

DON'T, CAN'T, WON'T, WOULDN'T, SHOULDN'T ALL USE AN APOSTROPHE WHERE A LETTER O SHOULD GO.

Level 2 Punctuation 2

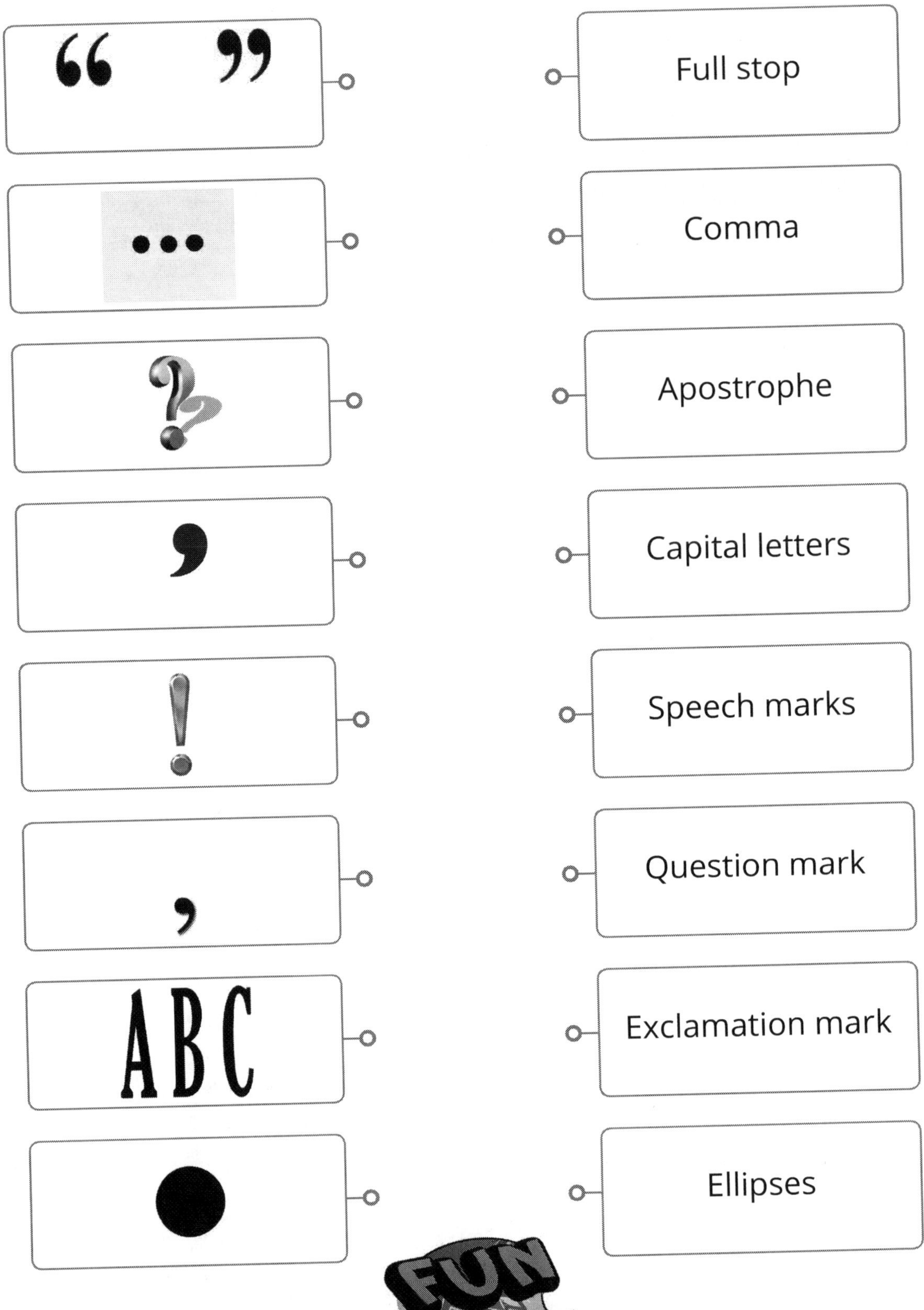

Level 2 Punctuation 3

1. creates a pause or breaks up ideas

   A ☐ ! exclamation marks

   B ☐ - dash

   C ☐ ? question mark

   D ☐ , commas

2. shows expression or importance

   A ☐ - dash

   B ☐ ; semi colon

   C ☐ ! exclamation marks

   D ☐ ... ellipsis

3. adds extra information which isn't necessarily needed

   A ☐ ; semi colon B ☐ ( ) brackets

   C ☐ ? question mark D ☐ ... ellipsis

4. signals a cliffhanger or shows words are missing

   A ☐ ... ellipsis B ☐ : colon

   C ☐ ( ) brackets D ☐ ' apostrophe

5. shows a question

   A ☐ ? question mark

   B ☐ ( ) brackets

   C ☐ ' ' inverted comma

   D ☐ ... ellipsis

6. used before a phrase which sums up a sentence or either side of a dropped in idea

   A ☐ ; semi colon B ☐ , commas

   C ☐ - dash D ☐ ! exclamation marks

7. introduces a list or links sentences that explain each other

   A ☐ : colon B ☐ - dash

   C ☐ ( ) brackets D ☐ ! exclamation marks

8. links two sentences often replacing and or but, seperates items in a long list

   A ☐ ! exclamation marks B ☐ ; semi colon

   C ☐ ( ) brackets D ☐ , commas

9. shows a word is informal or shows evidence from a text

   A ☐ ' apostrophe

   B ☐ ' ' inverted comma

   C ☐ ! exclamation marks

   D ☐ ( ) brackets

10. shows possession or a contraction

    A ☐ - dash

    B ☐ ' apostrophe

    C ☐ ' ' inverted comma

    D ☐ ... ellipsis

Level 2 Punctuation 4

Across

1. This shows that a sentence has ended (4,4)
5. used to show anger or excitement (11,4)
6. to replace a connective and separate two linked clauses (9)

Down

2. Used to separate clauses within a sentence (5)
3. At the end of an interrogative (8,4) *(Look it up in a dictionary)*
4. used for speech or quotations (6,5)
7. to introduce a list (5)

Level 2 Punctuation 5

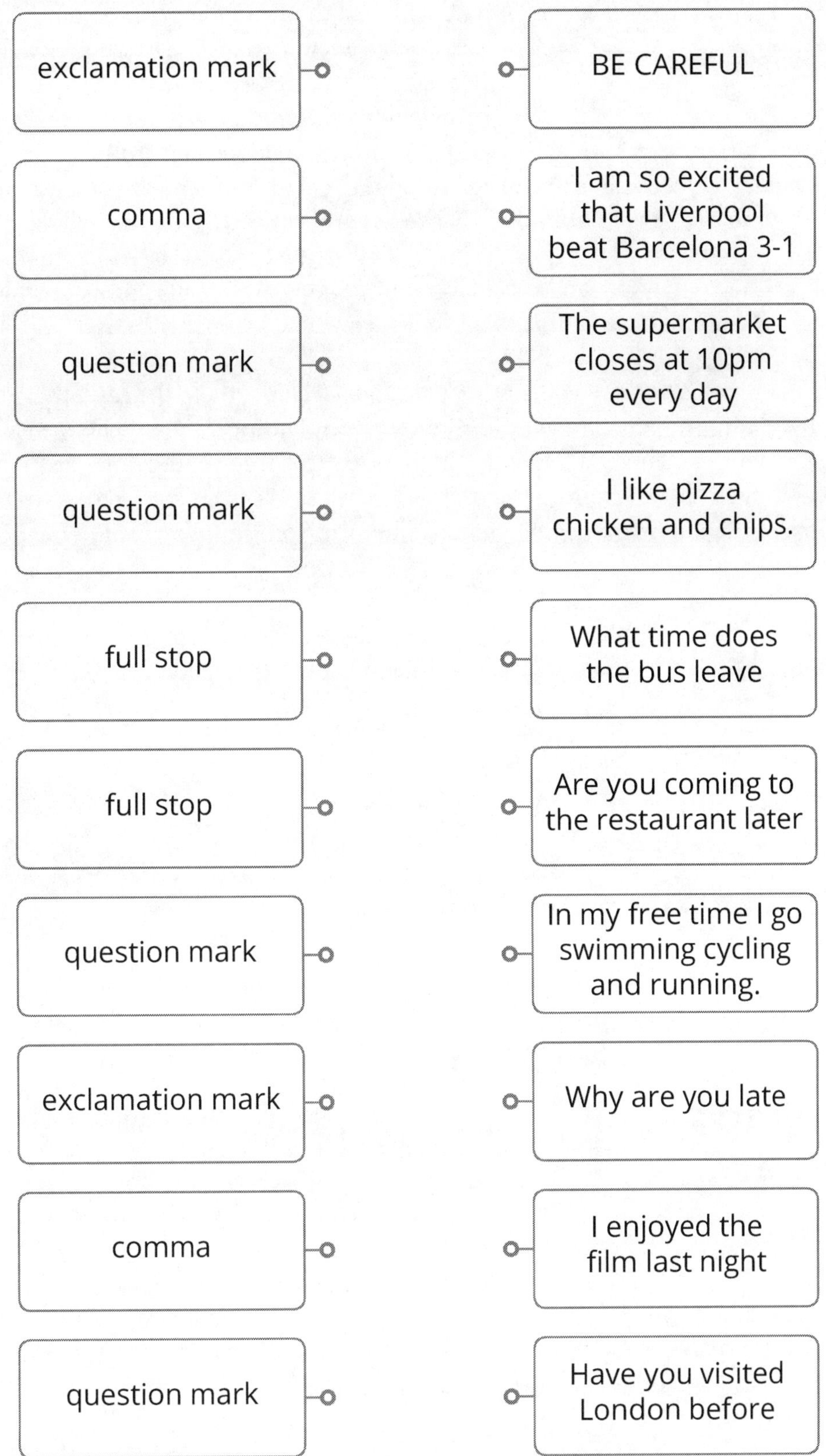

It might seem obvious, but the first thing before you do any form of writing is to identify your audience. Who will read this article, story, email, or press release? The answer to this question may well determine the form. If you need to ask your boss formally for a raise, you probably aren't going to write it in a Press Release. Hopefully, if you can't meet in person, you will send a professional-looking email. Similarly, if you have been put in charge of announcing a community Christmas carol concert, you may well decide to put up a few prominently placed posters, as well as issue a Press Release that might be sent to local and regional newspapers, as well as radio stations. An email is probably not the best method of communicating this event unless you attach a poster to it.

So, who is your audience? Are you aiming your message directly to the reader? For example, by sending an email to your boss, or, are you sending a Press Release to an online or newspaper editor, who you then expect to interpret the information and pass it on in some form, to the readers? In the latter, the information and form you present to the editor, will be different from the information and form you would present to members of the public.

Writing for your readership isn't just about knowing the form, or age demographic, it is about understanding every aspect of your audience. Some considerations are:

AGE
ETHNICITY
CULTURAL SENSITIVITIES
SEXUAL PREFERENCE OR IDENTITY
RELIGIOUS AFFILIATION
DISABILITIES OR SPECIAL NEEDS

Everything you read is written for a purpose. You need to figure out why it was written. Here's some reasons why people write:

Informative: The purpose of an informative text is to provide knowledge, facts, or explanations about a particular subject. It aims to educate or enlighten the reader. Examples include news articles, textbooks, and encyclopedias.

Persuasive: Persuasive texts aim to convince or persuade the reader to adopt a certain viewpoint, take specific action, or change their beliefs or behaviors. They often use persuasive techniques, logical arguments, and emotional appeals. Examples include opinion articles, advertisements, and political speeches.

Narrative: Narrative texts tell a story or recount a sequence of events. Their purpose is to entertain the reader through engaging characters, plot development, and descriptive language. Examples include novels, short stories, creative writingand memoirs.

Descriptive: Descriptive texts aim to create a vivid sensory experience for the reader by providing detailed descriptions of people, places, objects, or events. Their purpose is to paint a clear picture in the reader's mind. Examples include travel writing, poetry, and product descriptions. "It was a long, narrow road with trees overhanging."

Instructive: Instructive texts provide step-by-step guidance or directions on how to perform a task, operate a device, or complete a process. Their purpose is to inform and enable the reader to follow specific instructions. Examples include manuals, recipes, and tutorials. "Step One. Open the box."

Entertaining: The purpose of entertaining texts is to amuse, engage, or captivate the reader. They focus on providing enjoyment and escapism through humour, imaginative stories, or engaging content. Examples include jokes, comics, and entertaining articles.

It's important to note that texts can often serve multiple purposes simultaneously or have additional purposes specific to their intended audience or context. Here are some examples of kinds of texts and their purpose:

Advertisement: An advertisement is to promote a product, service, or brand and **persuade** the target audience to take a specific action, such as making a purchase, visiting a website, or subscribing to a service.

Editorial: An editorial is a type of text found in newspapers, magazines, or online publications. Its purpose is to **express the opinion** or viewpoint of the author or publication on a particular issue or topic. Editorials often aim to influence public opinion, spark discussion, or advocate for a specific position.

Social Media Post: Social media posts serve various purposes depending on the platform and context. They can be used to share **information**, engage with an audience, promote products or events, **entertain**, or inspire.

Personal Blog Post: A personal blog post is an informal type of text where the author shares personal experiences, thoughts, or opinions on a specific topic. The purpose can range from self-expression and storytelling to providing **advice**.

User Manual: A user manual is a text that provides **instructions** and guidance on how to use a product or service effectively. Its purpose is to **educate** users, clarify product features, and ensure users have a positive experience by understanding how to use the product or service correctly.

Level 2 Types of Text

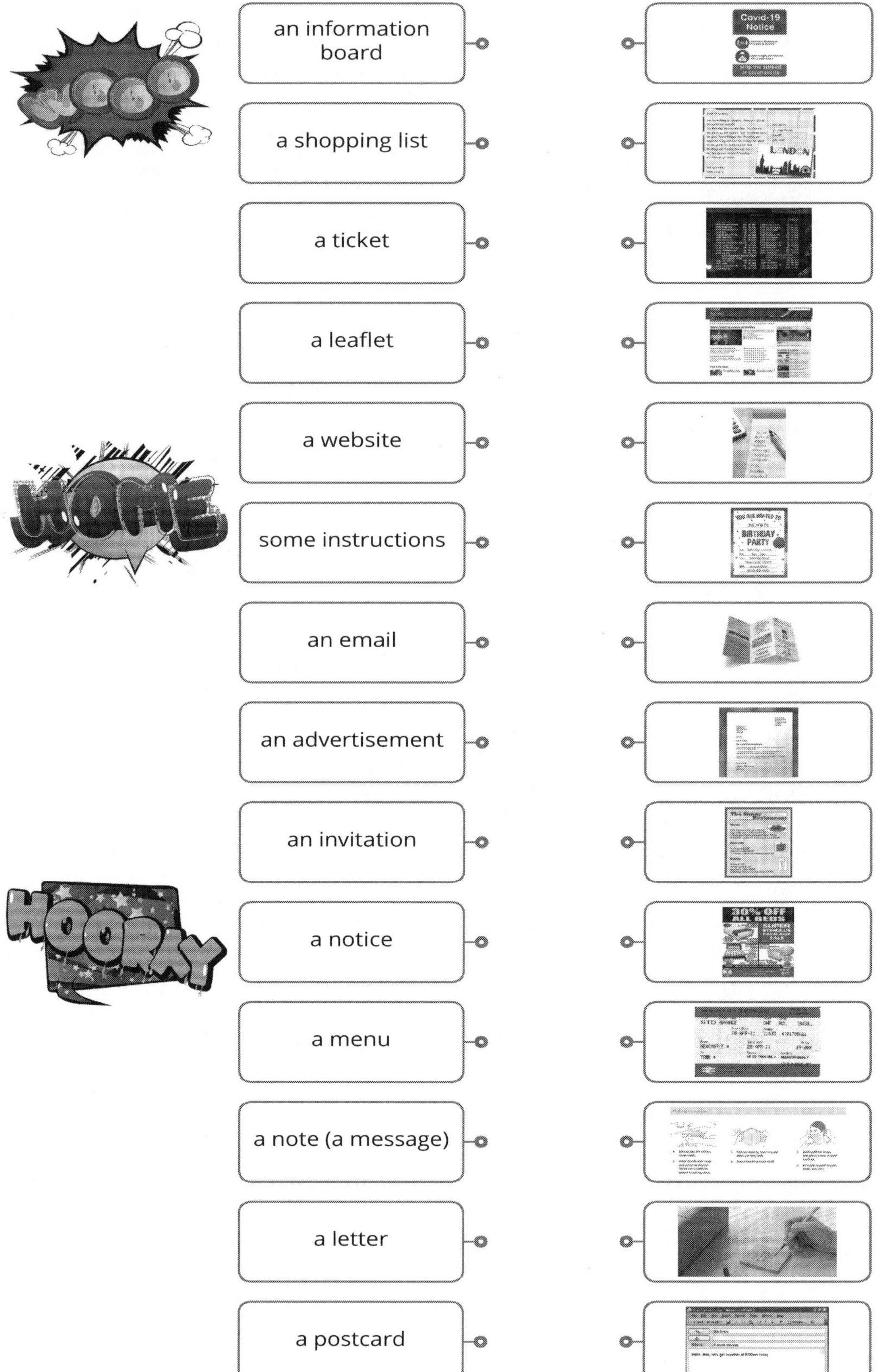

You need to be able to find information from texts that you read in everyday life. From newspapers, to online articles and social media, being able to read something and find what you are looking for is a skill you need to develop. Read this story and answer the questions.

In college, there was a boy named Alex who was pursuing a degree in computer science. He was known for his passion for coding and his exceptional problem-solving skills. Alex was actively involved in campus clubs related to technology and often participated in coding competitions. With his friendly and approachable nature, he made friends easily and was well-liked by his peers. In addition to his academic pursuits, Alex enjoyed playing the guitar and was a member of a local band that performed at college events. Despite the challenges of balancing his coursework and extracurricular activities, Alex remained dedicated to his studies and consistently achieved high grades.

Questions:

What degree is Alex pursuing in college? ....

What are two qualities that Alex is known for? ....

....

What kind of clubs is Alex involved in on campus? ....

....

What is one of Alex's hobbies outside of academics? ....

How does Alex perform in his studies? ....

....

Here's the answers.

Alex is pursuing a degree in computer science.
Alex is known for his passion for coding and exceptional problem-solving skills.
Alex is involved in campus clubs related to technology.
One of Alex's hobbies outside of academics is playing the guitar.
Alex consistently achieves high grades in his studies.

Skimming and scanning are two different reading techniques used to quickly gather information from a text. Here are the differences between skimming and scanning:

Skimming: Skimming involves quickly glancing over a text to get a general idea of its content. The purpose of skimming is to identify the main points, key ideas, and overall structure of the text. Skimming often involves reading headings, subheadings, topic sentences, and the first and last sentences of paragraphs. It helps in getting a quick overview of the text without reading every word.

Example: Skimming is useful when you want to preview a newspaper article to decide if it's worth reading. By quickly scanning the headline, subheadings, and the first few sentences of each paragraph, you can get a sense of the main topic and the key points discussed in the article.

Scanning: Scanning involves searching for specific information within a text. The purpose of scanning is to locate particular words, phrases, or pieces of information that are relevant to your specific needs or questions. Instead of reading the entire text, you focus on locating specific keywords or terms.

Example: Scanning is commonly used when searching for a specific name or date in a phone book or directory. You quickly move your eyes down the page, looking only for the specific information you need, while ignoring the rest of the content.

In summary, **skimming is used to quickly grasp the main ideas** and structure of a text, while **scanning is used to locate specific information** within a text. Both techniques are valuable for efficient reading and information retrieval, depending on the purpose and context of your reading task.

In an exam you may be given two or three different texts and you will be asked specific questions about each text. First, SKIM over the text looking for broad meaning, then SCAN the text looking for specific keywords associated with the question. For example: What are the **keywords** in these questions?

What does the author say you should give it each day to feed the horse a natural diet?
What does the text say are the uses for a plastic bucket on the farm?
How many minutes late was the train arriving at the station?

The keywords to scan for are 1. Natural Diet 2. Plastic Bucket 3. Late

If you scan the text looking for just the keywords, it will take you to the place where the rest of the answer can be found. This will save a lot of time.

Level 2 Skimming and scanning

Write in the item numbers in the list of boxes for each group

Scanning text

Skimming text

1 read more quickly

2 to obtain the gist - the overall sense - of a piece of writing.

3 • Look at the illustrations to give you more information about the topic.

4 decide if the text is interesting and whether you should read it in more detail

5 can help you decide whether to read it more slowly and in more detail

6 Read the title, subtitles and subheadings to find out what the text is about.

7 Don't try to read every word. Instead let your eyes move quickly across the page until you find what you're looking for.

8 If you're reading for study, start by thinking up or writing down some questions that you want to answer.

9 • Continue to think about the meaning of the text.

10 Used for browsing television schedules, timetables, lists, catalogues or webpages for information.

11 Used to read through the small ads in a newspaper,

12 You can use this technique to look up a phone number

13 Use clues on the page, such as headings and titles, to help you.

Writing a sentence should be straight forward, but many students struggle with some of the basics. A simple sentence always needs a **Subject** (the person or thing DOING the action) and a **Verb** (the action). Sentences may also have an **Object** (the receiver of the action - the one it is being done to).

So, every full sentence must have a DOER and an ACTION. **John** (the doer) **ate** (the action) **a cake** (the object or receiver of the action).

A sentence MUST start with a CAPITAL LETTER and end with a PERIOD. - unless

it ends with an exclamation mark! or a question mark? There are no excuses for not starting with a capital letter and ending with a full stop.

Active sentences are a fundamental aspect of good writing. Writing in the active voice can make your sentences more engaging, direct, and powerful. In contrast, passive sentences can make your writing seem vague, unenthusiastic, and confusing. Active sentences are those in which the **subject** of the sentence **performs the action**, while passive sentences are those in which the subject receives the action. For example:

Active sentence: The dog chased the ball.
Passive sentence: The ball was chased by the dog.

In the active sentence, the subject (the dog) is performing the action (chased), while in the passive sentence, the subject (the ball) is receiving the action (was chased).

Active sentences are often more concise and clear than passive sentences. Try to use them.

Passive sentence: The cake was eaten by the children.
Active sentence: The children ate the cake.

In your writing tasks try to put two sentences together to make one long sentence.
Use linking words (conjunctions) like: **AND, BUT or BECAUSE** (more on p15)

The team wrote the report and delivered it to the coach.

My brother drove the car, but he didn't have a license.

The author wrote the book because it had always been his dream.

IN LIFE, TRY TO WRITE LONGER SENTENCES AND USE LONGER WORDS. MAYBE CHALLENGE YOURSELF TO LEARN A NEW WORD EVERY DAY.

USE YOUR ACTIVE WRITING SKILLS TO REWRITE THESE PASSIVE SENTENCES. REMEMBER TO PUT THEM INTO SUBJECT - VERB - OBJECT ORDER.

Money was generously donated to the homeless shelter by Larry.

My sales ad was not responded to by anyone.

All the reservations will be made by the wedding planner.

For the bake sale, two dozen cookies will be baked by Susan.

The comet was viewed by the science class.

Every night the office is vacuumed and dusted by the cleaning crew.

The students questions are always answered by the Teacher

The entire stretch of road was paved by the workers.

The obstacle course was run by me in record time

LEARNING TO WRITE ACTIVELY IS A CHALLENGE. BUT THE MORE YOU PRACTICE, THE EASIER IT WILL BECOME.

Simple Sentence: A simple sentence consists of one independent clause, which means it contains a subject and a predicate and expresses a complete thought.

She sings beautifully.
The cat is sleeping.
I enjoy reading books.

Compound Sentence: A compound sentence consists of two or more independent clauses joined together by coordinating conjunctions - linking words - (such as "and," "but," or "or") or punctuation like a semicolon (;).

I like to swim, and my brother enjoys playing basketball.
She studied hard for the exam, but she still didn't get a good grade.
I can go to the party, or I can stay home and watch a movie.

Complex Sentence: A complex sentence contains one independent clause and at least one dependent clause. A dependent clause cannot stand alone as a complete sentence and relies on the independent clause for its meaning.

After I finish my work, I will go for a walk.
She started to cry when she heard the sad news.
Because it was raining, we decided to stay indoors.

What are conjunctions and connectives? They are words that connect words, phrases, or independent clauses of equal importance within a sentence. Think of them as words that join two short sentences together to make a longer one. Here is a list of the most common linking words.

Because: I went to the store **because** I needed some milk.
After: We went to the movies **after** we finished dinner.
As: She smiled at me **as** she walked by.
Before: Please finish your homework **before** you go out to play.
Since: He has been studying hard **since** he wants to pass the exam.
Unless: You won't succeed **unless** you work hard.
Until: We waited at the bus stop **until** the bus arrived.
While: She listened to music **while** she cleaned her room.
For: I bought some groceries, **for** I was planning to cook dinner.
And: She likes to read, **and** he enjoys playing video games.
Nor: He neither ate breakfast **nor** packed his lunch.
But: The weather was stormy, **but** they still decided to go for a walk.
Or: You can have coffee **or** tea with your breakfast.
Yet: The movie was long, **yet** we stayed until the end.
So: The car broke down, **so** we had to call for a tow truck.
As: She acted in the play **as** the lead character.
Nor: He didn't eat breakfast, **nor** did he pack his lunch.

Level 2 Conjunctions quiz

1. I didn't do my homework______________ my dog ate it!

   A ☐ because B ☐ so C ☐ and

2. It was sunny outside________________ we went out to play.

   A ☐ but B ☐ so C ☐ because

3. I was late ________________ my car didn't start.

   A ☐ and B ☐ but C ☐ because

4. I went to the shop________________ bought some fruit.

   A ☐ and B ☐ if C ☐ so

5. I opened the door _______________ someone was knocking.

   A ☐ but B ☐ and C ☐ because

6. Ben fell over ________________ he was not hurt.

   A ☐ but B ☐ because C ☐ if

7. The dog barked ________________ wagged his tail

   A ☐ because B ☐ so C ☐ and

8. I like apples _________________ I don't like oranges.

   A ☐ but B ☐ because C ☐ and

9. You should install street lights _____ it is safer.

   A ☐ so B ☐ but C ☐ and

10. You should install CCTV ___________ it will cost quite a lot of money.

    A ☐ because B ☐ although C ☐ so

11. You will get wet, ___ you go out in the rain

    A ☐ if B ☐ but C ☐ so

12. I had a great day, __________I felt tired in the evening.

    A ☐ so B ☐ because C ☐ although

13. We hoped to have a nice day: _____________the children were really naughty

    A ☐ so B ☐ however C ☐ and

14. I went to the reception ______ I arrived.

    A ☐ when B ☐ because C ☐ so

15. I mopped the floor _________ I stopped to have my lunch

    A ☐ but B ☐ because C ☐ before

CHECK THE CORRECT CONJUNCTION OR CONNECTIVE THAT BELONGS IN THE SPACE.

*** PRACTICE WRITING TWO SHORT SENTENCES THAT ARE RELATED, THEN JOIN THEM TOGETHER USING A CONJUNCTION/CONNECTIVE.**

"I WENT INTO THE ROOM AND I OPENED THE WINDOW."

AS YOU BEGIN TO DO THIS TRY USING THE MOST COMMON ONES:

REMEMBER - FANBOYS

FOR
AND
NOR
BUT
OR
YET
SO

IDENTIFY AND PUT A TICK UNDER EACH OF THE CONJUNCTIONS (LINKING WORDS)

Level 2 Sentence types

1. Curiosity killed the cat.

   A ☐ Simple sentence B ☐ Complex sentence C ☐ Compound sentence

2. The car swerved to miss Mrs Jackson, who had slipped off the pavement.

   A ☐ Simple sentence B ☐ Complex sentence C ☐ Compound sentence

3. I like tea, and he likes coffee.

   A ☐ Simple sentence B ☐ Complex sentence C ☐ Compound sentence

4. I always wanted to be somebody, but I should have been more specific.

   A ☐ Simple sentence B ☐ Complex sentence C ☐ Compound sentence

5. She ran quickly but still did not catch the escaping puppy

   A ☐ Simple sentence B ☐ Complex sentence C ☐ Compound sentence

6. She returned the computer after she noticed it was damaged.

   A ☐ Simple sentence B ☐ Complex sentence C ☐ Compound sentence

7. The movie, though very long, was still very enjoyable.

   A ☐ Simple sentence B ☐ Complex sentence C ☐ Compound sentence

Level 2 Complex Sentence

While I am a passionate basketball fan,	when the fireworks went off.
I nearly jumped out of my skin	I prefer rugby.
The boy walked home slowly	before starting the movie.
I always eat all my popcorn	since she retired.
Having a party is a bad idea	because the neighbours will complain.
My mum is extremely happy	he would be docked a day's pay.
As he was late again,	as he was feeling tired.
Whenever it rains,	I like to wear my blue coat.

Common grammatical errors can vary depending on the specific language and context, but here are some examples of frequent grammatical errors in English:

Improper use of capital letters: Remember that every sentence begins with a capital letter, and that proper nouns (names of places, people and things) should have a capital letter at the beginning. For example: Paris, France St Michael's Church Joan Smith

Subject-Verb Agreement: This error occurs when the subject and verb in a sentence do not match in terms of number (singular or plural). Example: "The dog chase the cat." (Incorrect) should be "The dog chases the cat." (Correct)

Misuse of Apostrophes: One common error is using apostrophes incorrectly in possessive forms or contractions. Example: "The cat's are playing in the yard." (Incorrect) should be "The cats are playing in the yard." (Correct). Do not add an apostrophe to make a word plural. For example, **do not write boy's** for the plural of boy. It is just boys.

Run-On Sentences: These occur when multiple independent clauses are incorrectly joined without appropriate punctuation or conjunctions. Example: "I went to the store I bought some groceries." (Incorrect) should be "I went to the store, and I bought some groceries." (Correct)

Sentence Fragments: These are incomplete sentences that lack a subject, verb, or complete thought. Example: "Running in the park on a sunny day." (Incorrect) should be "I enjoy running in the park on a sunny day." (Correct)

Incorrect Word Usage: Using the wrong word or confusing homophones (words that sound alike but have different meanings) can lead to errors. Example: "Their going to the party tonight." (Incorrect) should be "They're going to the party tonight." (Correct)

Lack of Agreement Between Pronouns and Antecedents (the thing that comes before or after): This error occurs when the pronoun does not match in terms of gender, number, or person. Example: "Each student should bring their own textbook." (Incorrect) should be "Each student should bring his or her own textbook." (Correct)

Grammar Quiz 1 **REWRITE THESE SENTENCES USING CORRECT GRAMMAR**

Incorrect: Me and my friend is going to the movies.

Incorrect: The book its cover is red.

Incorrect: I don't got no time to do my homework.

Incorrect: They was playing soccer in the park.

Incorrect: I seen that movie last night.

Incorrect: She don't want none of those cookies.

Incorrect: The cat laid on the couch all day.

Incorrect: I can't hardly wait for the party.

Incorrect: The students don't seems interested in the topic.

Incorrect: He don't know how to swim.

Grammar Quiz 2 **THIS STORY IS GRAMMATICALLY WRONG. TAKE YOUR TIME TO GO THROUGH EACH SENTENCE AND REWRITE THE STORY SO THAT IT IS GRAMMATICALLY CORRECT. TAKE YOUR TIME; THERE ARE A LOT OF ERRORS.**

Incorrect:
John is a college student. He study at a prestigious university in the city. Yesterday, John goes to the library to study for his upcoming exams. He sits at a table and takes out his textbook. John opens the book and begin to read. After a few minutes, his friends comes into the library. They sits next to him and starts talking loudly. John gets annoyed because he can't concentrate. He ask them to be quiet, but they ignores him.

Incorrect:
John decides to go for a walk to clear his minds. He walks through the campus and sees a group of students playing frisbee. He watch them for a while and thinks about joining, but he don't have a frisbee. John sees a friend across the field and waves at them. They waves back and calls him over. John walks towards them and they gives him a frisbee to join the game. They all have a lot of fun playing together.

Incorrect:
Later that evening, John goes to a coffee shop to meets his study group. They discusses their project and assign tasks to each other. John volunteers to writes the introduction while the others works on the research. They stays at the coffee shop for several hours, working hard on their assignments. Finally, they finishes their work and feels satisfied with their progress. They plans to meet again next week to finalize the project.

A QUICK REMINDER ABOUT WHEN TO USE CAPITAL LETTERS. IT IS VERY COMMON TO MISS CAPITALS. HERE ARE TEN EXAMPLES WHERE CAPITAL LETTERS SHOULD BE USED:

At the beginning of a sentence: "**T**he sun is shining brightly today."

For proper nouns: "I went to **P**aris last summer."

When referring to specific people: "**J**ohn is my best friend."

For the pronoun "I": "**I**'m not into sport, but **I** like to read books." (Big I not little i)

When addressing someone directly: "**H**ello, Sarah!"

In titles of books, movies, or songs: "I watched '**T**he **L**ord of the **R**ings' yesterday."

For the first word in a quotation: He said, "**L**ife is beautiful."

In names of organizations or institutions: "She works at the **U**nited **N**ations."

For days of the week and months of the year: "Our meeting is scheduled for **M**onday, **O**ctober 10th." But, not seasons! winter, spring, summer, autumn.

In the titles of formal documents or reports: "**T**he **A**nnual **R**eport of the **C**ompany."

Level 2 Capital letters

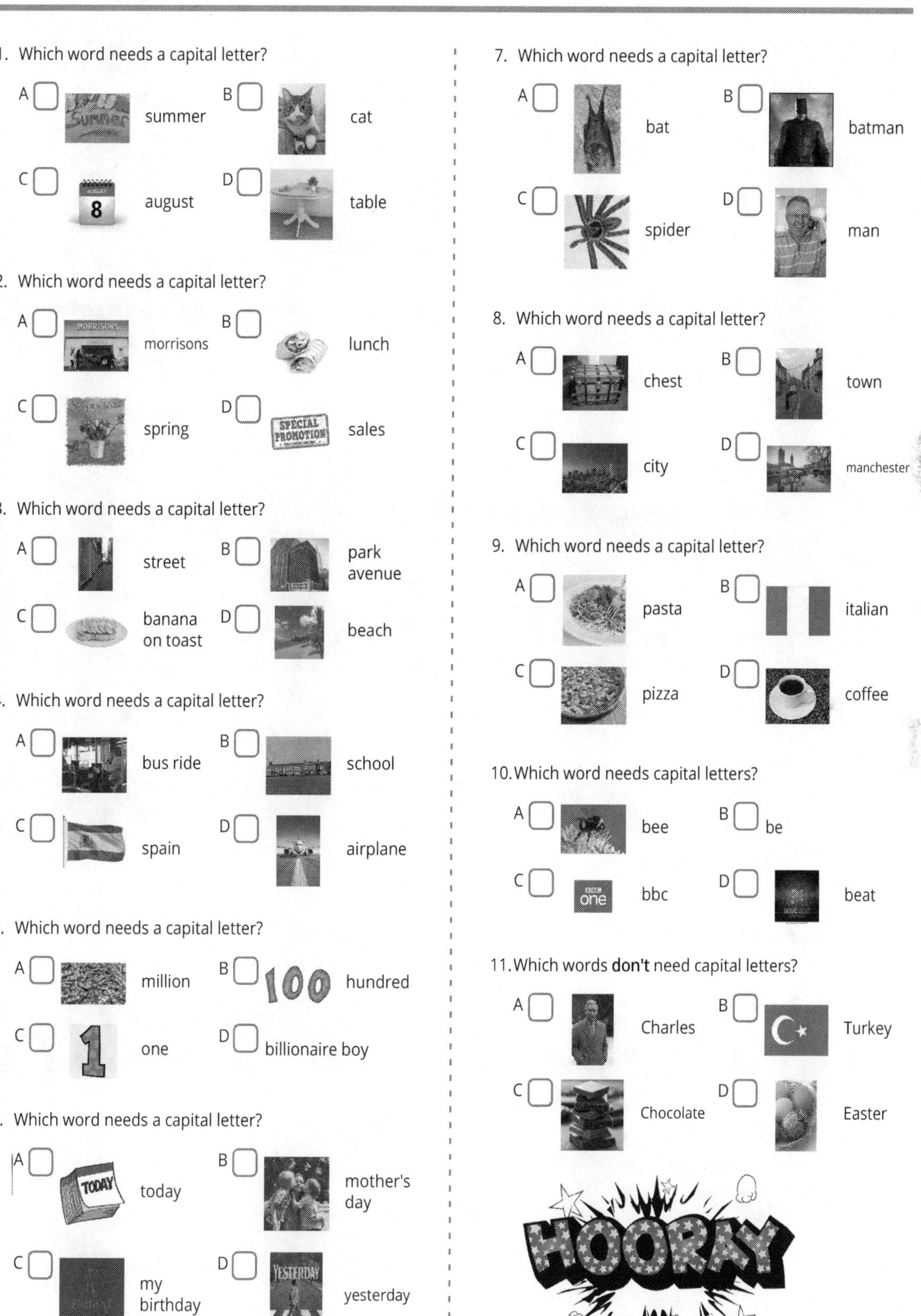

1. Which word needs a capital letter?

   A ☐ summer B ☐ cat
   C ☐ august D ☐ table

2. Which word needs a capital letter?

   A ☐ morrisons B ☐ lunch
   C ☐ spring D ☐ sales

3. Which word needs a capital letter?

   A ☐ street B ☐ park avenue
   C ☐ banana on toast D ☐ beach

4. Which word needs a capital letter?

   A ☐ bus ride B ☐ school
   C ☐ spain D ☐ airplane

5. Which word needs a capital letter?

   A ☐ million B ☐ hundred
   C ☐ one D ☐ billionaire boy

6. Which word needs a capital letter?

   A ☐ today B ☐ mother's day
   C ☐ my birthday D ☐ yesterday

7. Which word needs a capital letter?

   A ☐ bat B ☐ batman
   C ☐ spider D ☐ man

8. Which word needs a capital letter?

   A ☐ chest B ☐ town
   C ☐ city D ☐ manchester

9. Which word needs a capital letter?

   A ☐ pasta B ☐ italian
   C ☐ pizza D ☐ coffee

10. Which word needs capital letters?

   A ☐ bee B ☐ be
   C ☐ bbc D ☐ beat

11. Which words **don't** need capital letters?

   A ☐ Charles B ☐ Turkey
   C ☐ Chocolate D ☐ Easter

Level 2 Grammar Quiz 3

1. Which is correct?

   A ☐ To who should I give this report?　　B ☐ To whom should I give this report?

2. Which is correct?

   A ☐ A mediator is a disinterested party who helps people work out their differences.

   B ☐ A mediator is an uninterested party who helps people work out their differences.

3. Which is correct?

   A ☐ Lie that remote control down and get right to work on your chores!

   B ☐ Lay that remote control down and get right to work on your chores!

4. Which is correct?

   A ☐ It's time to go.　　B ☐ Its time to go.

5. Which is correct?

   A ☐ Elizabeth was stopped by a cop while running late for a meeting

   B ☐ While running late for a meeting, Elizabeth was stopped by a cop.

6. Which is correct?

   A ☐ Mr. Smith suffers from AD (e.g., Alzheimer's disease).

   B ☐ Mr. Smith suffers from AD (i.e., Alzheimer's disease).

HOORAY

7. Which is correct?

   A ☐ We'll get much farther if we can talk about this rationally.

   B ☐ We'll get much further if we can talk about this rationally.

KNOW YOUR HOMOPHONES! THESE ARE WORDS THAT SOUND THE SAME, BUT HAVE DIFFERENT SPELLING, AND DIFFERENT MEANINGS, LIKE WHERE AND WEAR. IT IS IMPORTANT TO KNOW HOMOPHONES - HOW TO SPELL THEM - AND HOW THEY DIFFER IN MEANING.

Level 2 Homophones Crossword

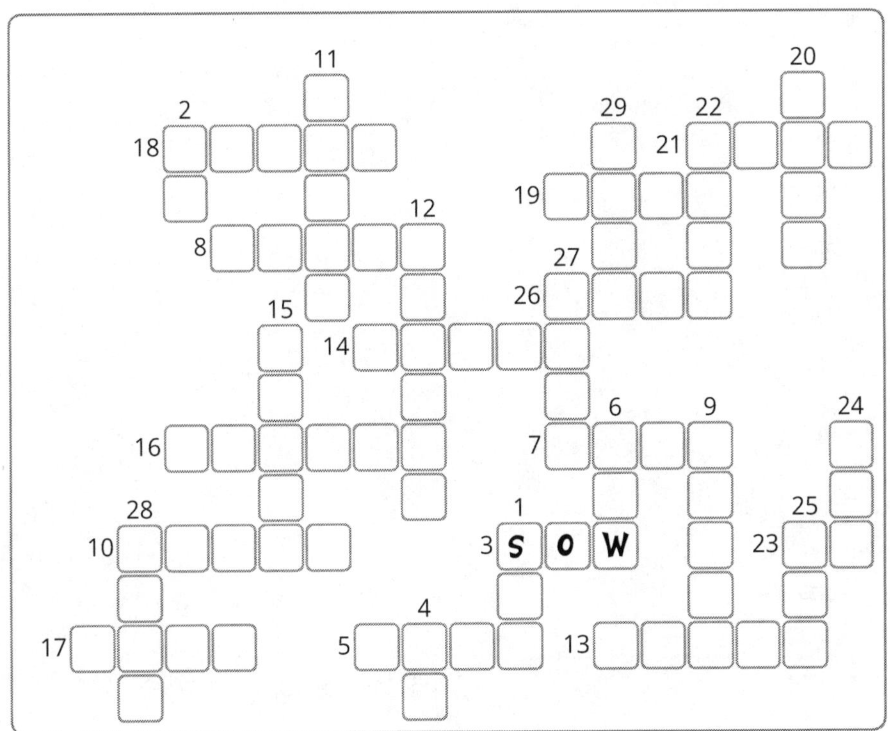

Across
3. pig (3)
5. am aware of (4)
7. was aware of (4)
8. at the top of the legs (5)
10. location (5)
13. slice of cake (5)
14. no war (5)
16. a pretty plant (6)
17. the land you build on (4)
18. being able to see (5)
19. gender (4)
21. not strong (4)
23. alongside (2)
26. dripping tap (4)

Down
1. with a needle (3)
2. therefore (2)
4. in the negative (2)
6. first appearance (3)
9. rubbish (5)
11. belonging to them (5)
12. they are (7)
15. ingredient (5)
20. post (4)
22. 7 days (4)
24. purchase (3)
25. farewell (3)
27. welsh vegetable (4)
28. dogs wag them (4)
29. story (4)

Level 2 Homophones Quiz

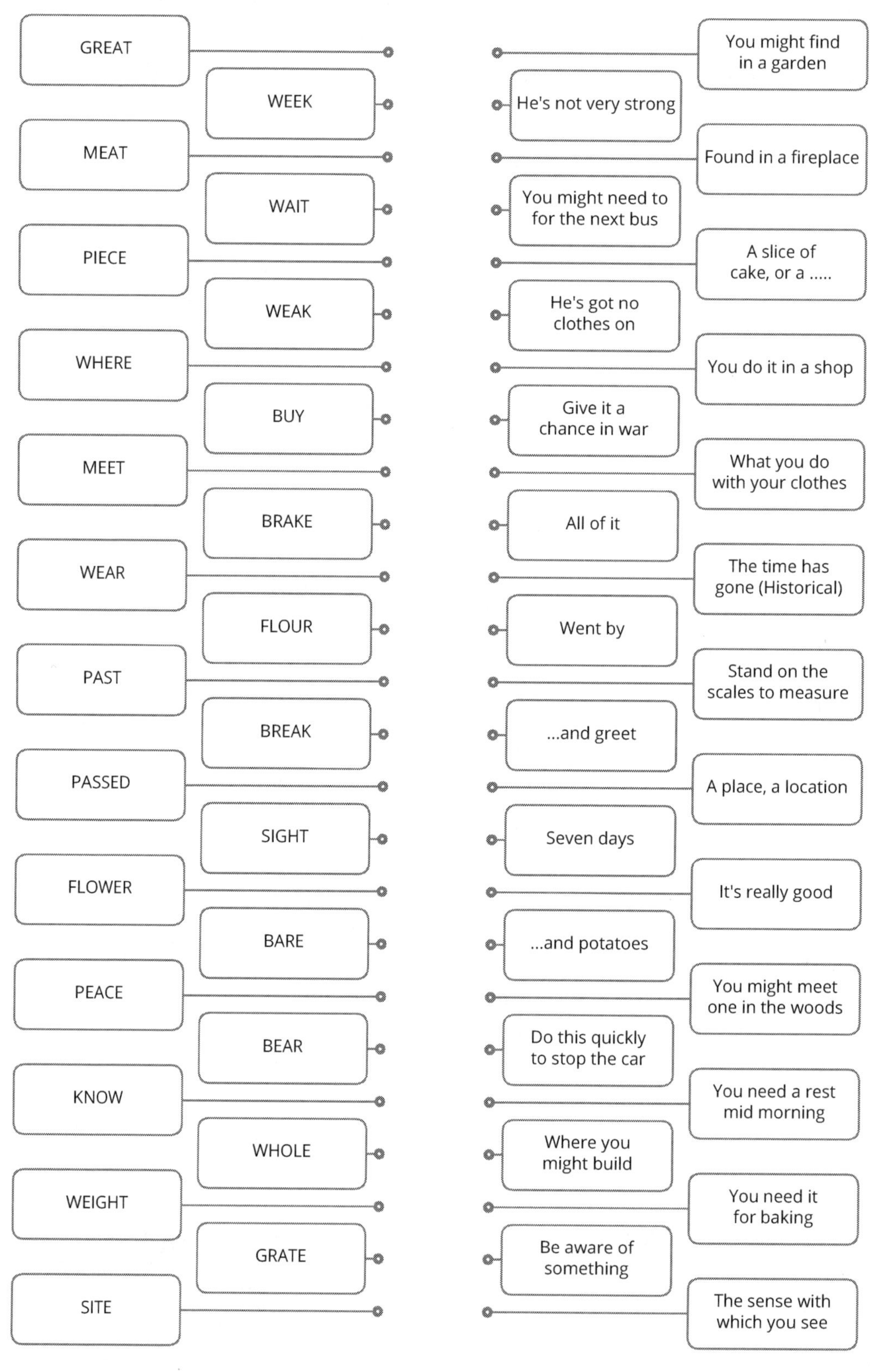

SYNONYMS ARE WORDS THAT HAVE SIMILAR MEANINGS, LIKE 'GREAT AND GOOD,' LIKE 'WELL DONE' AND 'CONGRATULATIONS' - SIMILAR MEANINGS. BUT ANTONYMS ARE WORDS THAT HAVE OPPSITE MEANINGS, LIKE 'GOOD AND BAD' - BAD IS AN ANTONYM OF GOOD. 'HOT' IS AN ANTONYM OF 'COLD' - OPPOSITE MEANINGS. SEE IF YOU CAN MATCH UP THESE SYNONYMS.

Level 2 Synonyms Quiz (SIMILAR MEANINGS)

nervous	courageous
hungry	breakable
dark	ravenous
fragile	gloomy
thirsty	dazzling
rich	feeble
brave	anxious
strong	parched
bright	powerful
weak	wealthy

Level 2 Dictionary Corner - Use a dictionary to find a word with a similar meaning **(DO NOT GUESS! THIS EXERCISE IS TO GET YOU USED TO USING A DICTIONARY)**

1. The **diligent** student received an A on the exam.

A ☐ hardworking B ☐ apathetic C ☐ lazy

2. The detective **carefully** examined the crime scene.

A ☐ haphazardly B ☐ carelessly C ☐ meticulously

3. The chef prepared a **delicious** meal for the guests.

A ☐ tasteless B ☐ tasty C ☐ repulsive

4. The athlete demonstrated exceptional **agility** during the game.

A ☐ nimbleness B ☐ clumsiness C ☐ sluggishness

5. The teacher used **innovative** methods to engage the students.

A ☐ conventional B ☐ outdated C ☐ creative

6. The speaker delivered a **persuasive** argument to the audience.

A ☐ nonsensical B ☐ compelling C ☐ incoherent

7. The artist exhibited her **stunning** artwork at the gallery.

A ☐ unimpressive B ☐ mediocre C ☐ impressive

8. The scientist conducted **extensive** research for the project.

A ☐ thorough B ☐ superficial C ☐ incomplete

9. The team **collaborated** effectively to complete the task.

A ☐ competed B ☐ cooperated C ☐ conflicted

10. The author crafted a **captivating** story that kept readers hooked.

A ☐ uninteresting B ☐ tedious C ☐ engrossing

DO NOT GOOGLE! USING A DICTIONARY IS A SKILL YOU NEED TO LEARN FOR LIFE. IT WILL HELP YOU AS YOU FIND WORDS ALPHABETICALLY.

Level 2 Antonyms Quiz (OPPOSITE MEANINGS)

REMEMBER THAT ANTONYMS ARE WORDS THAT MEAN THE OPPOSITE. SEE IF YOU CAN MATCH THESE OPPOSITE WORDS. LET'S SEE HOW GOOD YOU ARE!

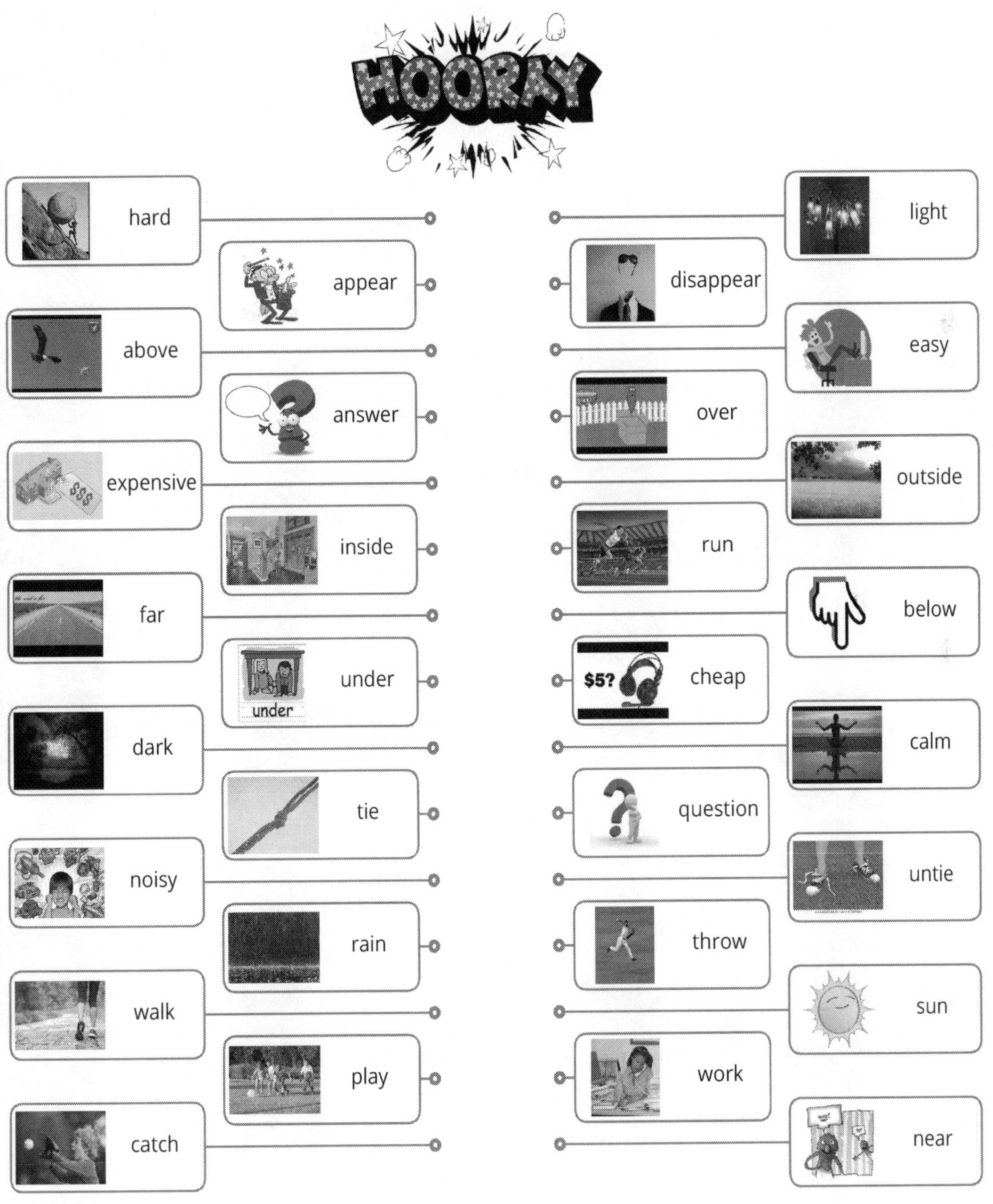

Inference is about reading between the lines to figure out what is going on. If you see someone walking with an umbrella, it is safe to assume they might be expecting it to rain today. Nobody told you that, but you figured it out from the information you were given. Similarly, you can look at an image and probably tell me what time of day it is without anyone telling you. Inference is all about looking at the information you are given, trying to gather clues, and infer from what you read or see - something that is not stated. It's like being a detective of words.

Look at these two examples below. What can be inferred by reading each of these paragraphs in a story? You're not looking for the things the story tells you directly, you are looking for what it implies.

Example 1:
The restaurant was filled with the savoury aroma of spices and sizzling meat. Patrons sat at candlelit tables, their faces illuminated by the warm glow. The clinking of cutlery and soft murmurs of conversation filled the air. The waiter briskly moved from table to table, serving plates of steaming dishes. In the corner, a musician strummed a guitar, adding a melodic backdrop to the ambiance.

Tell us something that the paragraph doesn't say ....

....

Example 2:
The alarm blared loudly, jolting Sarah awake from her sleep. She quickly checked the time—6:30 AM. With a groan, she reluctantly swung her legs over the side of the bed and stumbled towards the bathroom. The sound of running water soon followed as she brushed her teeth and splashed her face with cold water. Sarah hastily got dressed, grabbed a granola bar, and rushed out the door.

Tell us something the paragraph doesn't say ....

....

Inference 1: The restaurant provides a cozy and intimate dining experience. The use of candlelit tables and live music suggests it is an upscale establishment with a pleasant atmosphere.

(These are only examples of answers. Yours are probably also correct)

Inference 2: Sarah overslept and had to rush to get ready for the day. The alarm and her groan indicate that she was not ready to wake up, and her actions of brushing her teeth, splashing her face, and grabbing a granola bar suggest a limited amount of time for morning routines.

Level 2 Inference vocabulary

Across

3. It is i_____ that the boys are used to strict discipline at school. (7)
4. The i___________ is that everyone has to conform. (11)
5. Holmes d________ that the woman was unhappily married. (7)
7. Those are the facts; what do you c______ from them? _____ (8)

Down

1. From the expression on his face, I s____ that something bad had happended. (8)
2. What are you i_____ by that remark? (9)
6. He d________ great pleasure from painting. (7)
8. Holmes made a d_______ regarding Watson himself. (9)

READ THE SENTENCES AND WORK OUT THE MISSING INFERENCE LANGUAGE WORDS THAT GO IN THE CROSSWORD PUZZLE.

Level 2 Inference Quiz

HOW GOOD ARE YOU AT READING BETWEEN THE LINES? LOOK AT THE CLUES ON THE RIGHT AND MATCH THEM UP TO WHAT YOU THINK IS GOING ON IN THE LEFT COLUMN. THE CLUES ON THE RIGHT LEAD YOU TO INFER THAT SOMETHING MAY BE HAPPENING ON THE LEFT.

The teacher is nervous and is waiting for something to happen.	The boy is walking down the road with red eyes, wet cheeks and their head down.
The teacher is going on holiday.	The character is smiling.
The boy is sad and has been crying.	The character's head is staring at a book while he is writing.
The character is happy.	The teacher is packing her sun hat and sun cream into a suitcase.
The character is diligent.	The student's fists are clenched together and their face is red.
The student is angry.	A teacher is pacing up and down and keeps looking at her watch.

What on earth are organizational features or organizational techniques? These are two terms educators use. They just mean LAYOUT. They are referring to the way the information is set out on the page.

Some examples of organizational features are:

Paragraphs - Headings/Titles - Italics Sub Headings - Bullet Points - Images - Captions - Text Boxes - Chronological Order - Tables - Graphs - Charts - Bold Text - Numbered List - Speech Bubble

Think about ways the author of a the text has chosen to lay out their writing - so that it is easier to read and understand. Organizational features make it easier to read by adding visual elements to break up the writing.

When reading, try to **Identify what organizational features the writer has used in the text.** Make sure you know the many ways text can be organized. Look at a typical newspaper or an advert and all the ways the publisher uses to get the information across in a visually pleasing way. There might be a headline, maybe a sub heading, a large image with a caption, quotes may be separated into a box, and there may be charts showing facts or statistics.

When using these organizational features you must think about your audience. 'Who is reading what I am writing?' Then, you can determine what elements will help your readers understand your message more clearly. If you are writing a scientific journal then using data charts and graphs may be helpful. If you are writing a children's book, then lots of images and illustrations are necessary.

Instead of a weather person just reading what the weather forecast is going to be over the next few days, they use a map of the country, with symbols showing if it is going to be sunny, or rainy, and they have numbers on the screen indicating high and low temperatures. They may even have arrows indicating wind direction. These visual elements are similar to what a writer would use to explain the text.

Ask yourself, **"Why has the author used these organizational features?"** Be prepared to look at text with a critical eye, and understand the reasoning behind using different layout features. Answers may include: 'to make it stand out' 'to highlight that point' 'to make it easier to read' 'to give a visual example of rising prices.'

ORGANIZATIONAL FEATURES QUIZ

1. Small symbols, often black circles, used to list items

A ☐ speech bubble B ☐ paragraph

C ☐ bullet points D ☐ webpage tab

2. A box with a border (separate from the main text)

A ☐ title/heading B ☐ text box

C ☐ bullet points D ☐ column

3. Additional information at the bottom of the page

A ☐ text box B ☐ image

C ☐ footnote D ☐ home icon

4. A box with rows and columns (containing information)

A ☐ table B ☐ browser bar

C ☐ column D ☐ bullet points

5. Words which are darker/heavier

A ☐ column B ☐ hyperlink

C ☐ bold font D ☐ browser bar

6. Inform the reader what the text is about

A ☐ browser bar B ☐ bold font

C ☐ title/heading D ☐ italics

7. Inform the reader what a section is about

A ☐ bullet points B ☐ caption

C ☐ subheading D ☐ column

8. A shape containing a quote (spoken words)

A ☐ speech bubble B ☐ subheading

C ☐ italics D ☐ bullet points

9. Items are numbered (instructions or list)

A ☐ numbered list B ☐ browser bar

C ☐ footnote D ☐ text box

10. A picture, drawing or photograph

A ☐ browser bar B ☐ column

C ☐ table D ☐ image

11. Words which explain an image used in a text

A ☐ hyperlink B ☐ caption

C ☐ subheading D ☐ numbered list

12. You click on this to jump to another page or document

A ☐ table B ☐ image

C ☐ hyperlink D ☐ caption

ORGANIZATIONAL FEATURES LEAFLET

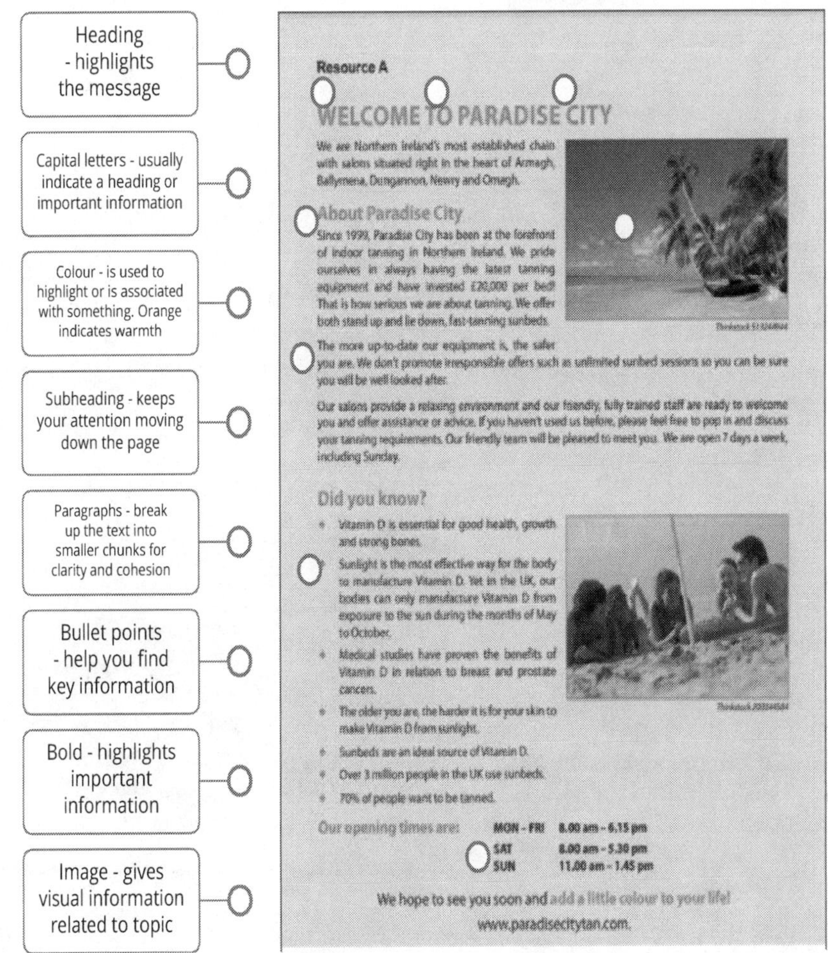

Organizational features help break down the content into manageable sections. This improves clarity and comprehension by presenting information in a structured way, allowing the audience to quickly grasp key points and understand the message being conveyed.

By using organizational features, you can create a visual hierarchy that guides the reader's attention. Headings and subheadings draw attention to important information, while bullet points and numbered lists emphasize key features or benefits. This helps the audience navigate through the text, focus on relevant details, and absorb the main points effectively.

In today's fast-paced world, many people skim or scan rather than reading texts word-for-word. Organizational features make it more readable and scannable by breaking it into digestible chunks. This allows the audience to quickly locate specific information of interest, increasing engagement and reducing the chances of them losing interest or becoming overwhelmed. Make sure you know the features and why they are used.

ORGANIZATIONAL FEATURES QUIZ

- Heading
- Bullet points
- Text Box
- Image
- Foot note
- Bold text
- Italics

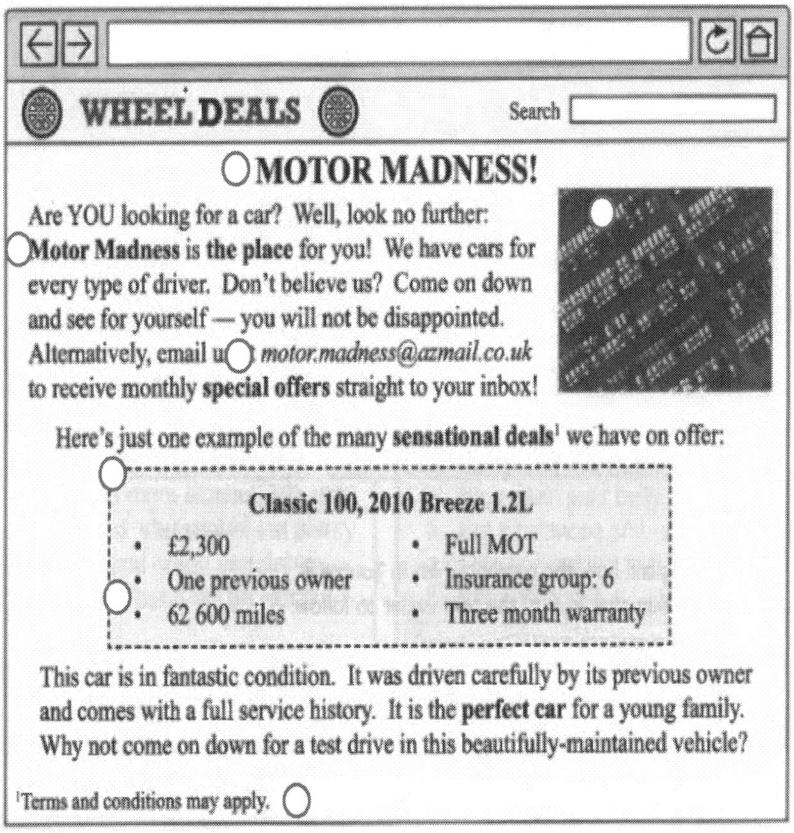

WHEEL DEALS

Search

MOTOR MADNESS!

Are YOU looking for a car? Well, look no further: **Motor Madness is the place** for you! We have cars for every type of driver. Don't believe us? Come on down and see for yourself — you will not be disappointed. Alternatively, email us *motor.madness@azmail.co.uk* to receive monthly **special offers** straight to your inbox!

Here's just one example of the many **sensational deals**[1] we have on offer:

Classic 100, 2010 Breeze 1.2L

- £2,300
- One previous owner
- 62 600 miles
- Full MOT
- Insurance group: 6
- Three month warranty

This car is in fantastic condition. It was driven carefully by its previous owner and comes with a full service history. It is the **perfect car** for a young family. Why not come on down for a test drive in this beautifully-maintained vehicle?

[1]Terms and conditions may apply.

REMEMBER, THE TERMS ORGANIZATIONAL FEATURES AND ORGANIZATIONAL TECHNIQUES MEAN THE SAME THING - LAYOUT. WHAT METHODS DOES THE AUTHOR USE TO LAYOUT THE TEXT - AND WHY DO THEY USE THEM? HOW ARE YOU AFFECTED BY THE WAY SOMEONE LAYS OUT AN ADVERT, ARTICLE, OR EVEN A SOCIAL MEDIA POST?

Choosing the right format when you write is essential. You probably send text messages to your friends, using 'text speak.' But, in the business world, or just in everyday life, you may be asked to write a letter or an email. Yes, people do still write letters! These will probably be very formal, perhaps a letter to the local council, or an email to a business assoicate. Whatever you are asked to write, you need to know the format, and know it well. For this book, we will just concentrate on a few, like the formal letter and the formal email, but you may also be asked to write a review or an eyewitness report. Look up the format of each so that you are prepared. Please note that although the format differs with each, the content is very similar in how it is set out.

When writing, we follow an IPPPC format. This means that, after deciding the style (letter, email, post) at the top of your document correct, the body of your text will go as follows:

INTRODUCTION - This is where you get to the point of your communication. Why are you writing this letter or email? You do not need to say, "Hello, I'm Patrick...." Your name is already on the letter or email - so don't write that. Also, DON'T WRITE, "I am writing to you because.... Or, "I am sending you this email because." They have the letter or email in front of them, so you don't need to explain what it is...get right to the point.

"I would like to apply for the job as caretaker at your college......"
"I would like to apply for a scholarship....."

PARAGRAPH 1 - This is where you outline the situation. Give facts here. Tell about the night you visited their restaurant, about the dinner served, about what happened that caused you to write.

PARAGRAPH 2 - This is where you elaborate and give more evidence, more information, where you build your case, or tell more about yourself and your qualifications.

PARAGRAPH 3 - This is where you might talk about how this situation made you and your group FEEL. Yes, you can bring emotion in here. What affect did the situation have upon you?

CONCLUSION or CALL TO ACTION - This is where you tell the person what you want to happen next. What do you want them to do, and by when? Do they need to respond to your request within so many days? Can they call you? If so, be sure to put your phone number at the bottom of the message.

Although we are asking you to write an intro, followed by three paragraphs and a conclusion - it really isn't too much. Aim for a total of perhaps 250 to 300 words. That should give you room to cover all the bases, and get your message across. Practice writing 300 word letters, emails, articles, reviews, reports etc.

Letter Level 2 Quiz

HAVE A GO, THEN CHECK FOR THE RIGHT FORMAT AT THE BACK OF THE BOOK.

Draw a line from each of the elements of the letter to the position they should go.

HERE IS A LETTER FOR YOU TO FORMAT. DRAW YOUR LINES IN PENCIL, AND HAVE A GO. IT MAY TAKE YOU A FEW TIMES BEFORE YOU GET ALL THE FORMAT ELEMENTS IN THE RIGHT ORDER. YOU WILL NEED TO KNOW THIS EXACT FORMAT.

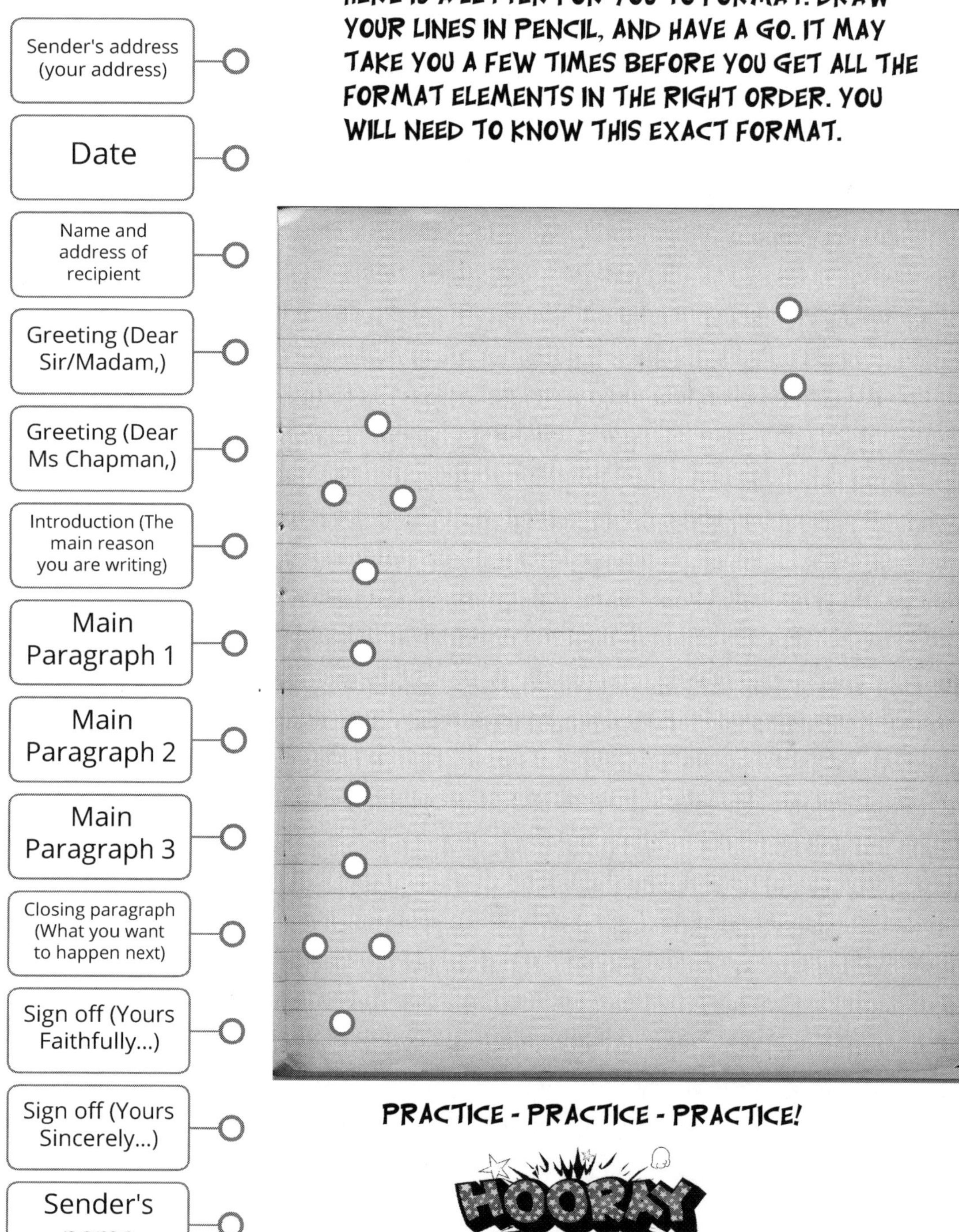

PRACTICE - PRACTICE - PRACTICE!

HOORAY

IF YOU KNOW THE NAME OF THE RECIPIENT, USE IT WHEN WRITING DEAR..... THEN, END WITH YOURS SINCERELY. IF YOU DON'T KNOW THE NAME, USE DEAR SIR/MADAM... AND ALWAYS END WITH YOURS FAITHFULLY. EMAILS SHOULD ALWAYS END WITH REGARDS, OR KIND REGARDS.

Level 2 Letter Writing Quiz

1. A letter written to a friend is known as

   A ☐ a formal letter

   B ☐ a business letter

   C ☐ an informal letter

   D ☐ a letter of application

2. The first item on the top right of a letter is

   A ☐ the recipient's address

   B ☐ reference to what you are writing about

   C ☐ the greeting or salutation

   D ☐ sender's address

3. You should greet your friend as

   A ☐ Dear Sir

   B ☐ Dear..........(surname)

   C ☐ Dear ....(first name)

   D ☐ Dear Madam

4. The information that follows in your letter should be written

   A ☐ in paragraphs

   B ☐ in columns

   C ☐ a chapter

   D ☐ one block

5. You begin a new paragraph when

   A ☐ you start a new sentence

   B ☐ you change to a new idea

   C ☐ you have more of the same information

   D ☐ you explain a point

6. You close an informal letter with

   A ☐ yours sincerely

   B ☐ yours faithfully

   C ☐ love/best wishes

   D ☐ yours in hope

WHOOOSH

OFFICIAL LETTERS AND EMAILS ALWAYS REQUIRE YOU TO USE FORMAL LANGUAGE.

NEVER EXPRESS YOUR ANGER IN A LETTER OR EMAIL. IT WILL NOT GET YOU WHAT YOU WANT, AND WILL UPSET THE RECIEVER - MAKING THEM LESS EAGER TO HELP SOLVE YOUR PROBLEM.

BE FIRM - BUT POLITE. UNDERSTAND AND EXPRESS BOTH SIDES OF THE ARGUMENT.

FORMAL EMAIL LAYOUT QUIZ

REMEMBER TO USE THE IPPC FORMAT

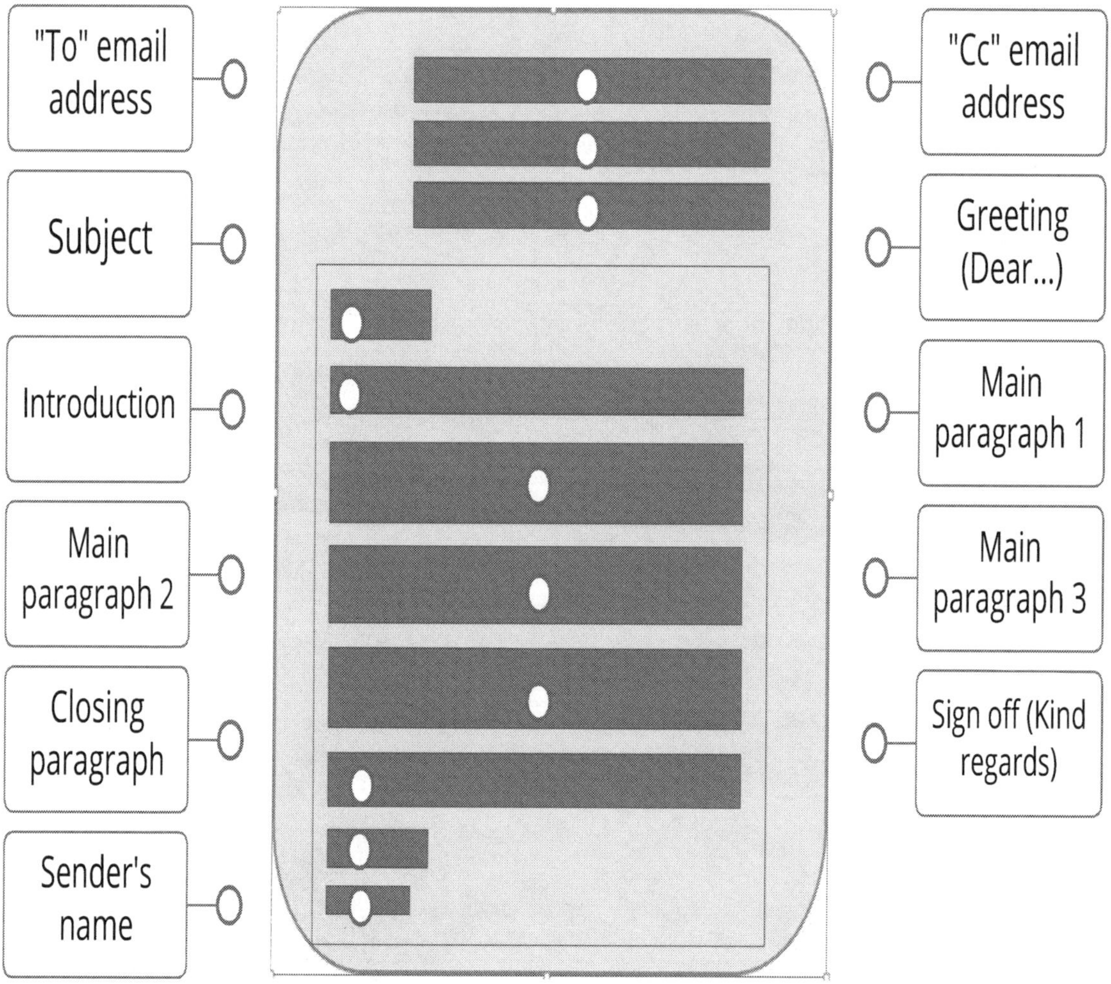

"To" email address

Subject

Introduction

Main paragraph 2

Closing paragraph

Sender's name

"Cc" email address

Greeting (Dear...)

Main paragraph 1

Main paragraph 3

Sign off (Kind regards)

DO NOT FORGET TO FILL OUT THE SUBJECT LINE OF THE EMAIL. THIS IS A COMMON ERROR.

ALSO, DO NOT SIGN OFF WITH 'YOURS SINCERELY' OR 'YOURS FAITHFULLY' - EMAILS SHOULD ALWAYS END WITH EITHER 'REGARDS' OR 'KIND REGARDS.'

LAYOUT OF A REVIEW

Heading

Introduction with facts

Including some descriptive language to add to the facts

Information about the songs with colourful descriptions

Rhetorical question

Particular/peculiar information about album

Writer's opinion

My Top Choice

I'm certainly not alone in my choice of favourite album. In fact, Michael Jackson's "Thriller" has sold over 50 million copies worldwide since being released in 1982, and still currently holds the much-coveted title of "best-selling album of all time". A toe-tapping blend of pop, funk, and R&B, it's sure to get everyone grooving at a party, yet also contains unexpected emotional power in the lyrics.

Jam-packed full of catchy melodies such as the opening the famous "Beat it" and "Wanna be startin something", almost every song makes you want to hum along. It's like a feast for the ears, with a range of styles from the soft duet ballad with Paul McCartney "The Girl is Mine" to the rock/pop of the title track. The album will leave you with no doubt of the unique and extraordinary talent of the King of Pop. What disco would be complete without a few of his renowned numbers?

Unlike much of today's modern pop, this album actually deals with a huge number of deep themes such as jealousy, loneliness and obsession. The song "Billie Jean", for example, chronicles a story of a crazed fan who insists that she has his baby. Not hard to imagine that the artist was channelling some real experiences in his writing.

It doesn't surprise me at all that this remains the best-selling album of all time and I challenge ever the most cynical listener to play "Thriller" without tapping along.

A Review should contain the following elements:

Introduction:
Start your review with a clear and concise introduction that provides an overview of what you will be reviewing. Include the name of the product, service, or subject of the review, and provide some context or background information if necessary. State your overall opinion or thesis statement.

Body:
It should contain the main content and analysis. Here are a few elements to consider:

a. Organization: Organize your review into logical paragraphs or sections. Each paragraph should focus on a specific aspect or feature of the subject being reviewed.

b. Description: Provide a thorough and objective description of the product or service. Include relevant details such as appearance, functionality, performance, or any other pertinent characteristics.

c. Evaluation: Offer your evaluation and analysis of the subject based on your personal experience or expertise. Discuss both positive and negative aspects, highlighting strengths and weaknesses.

d. Examples: Support your evaluation with specific examples or anecdotes. Use real-life scenarios, experiences, or observations to illustrate your points and make your review more relatable.

e. Comparison: If applicable, compare the subject of the review to similar products or services in the market. This can provide additional context and help readers understand the relative merits or drawbacks.

Conclusion:
End your review with a concise summary of your main points and a clear overall opinion or recommendation. Restate your thesis statement from the introduction and provide a final assessment or verdict.

Ratings or Scores (optional):
If appropriate, you may choose to include a rating system or scores to provide a quick summary of your evaluation. This can be in the form of stars, numerical ratings, or a scale. Ensure that you explain the criteria or basis for your ratings to give readers a better understanding of your judgment.

Call to Action (optional):
Depending on the purpose of your review, you may include a call to action. This can be a suggestion to try out the product, visit a website, or take any other relevant action based on your evaluation.

Level 2 Writing an Application

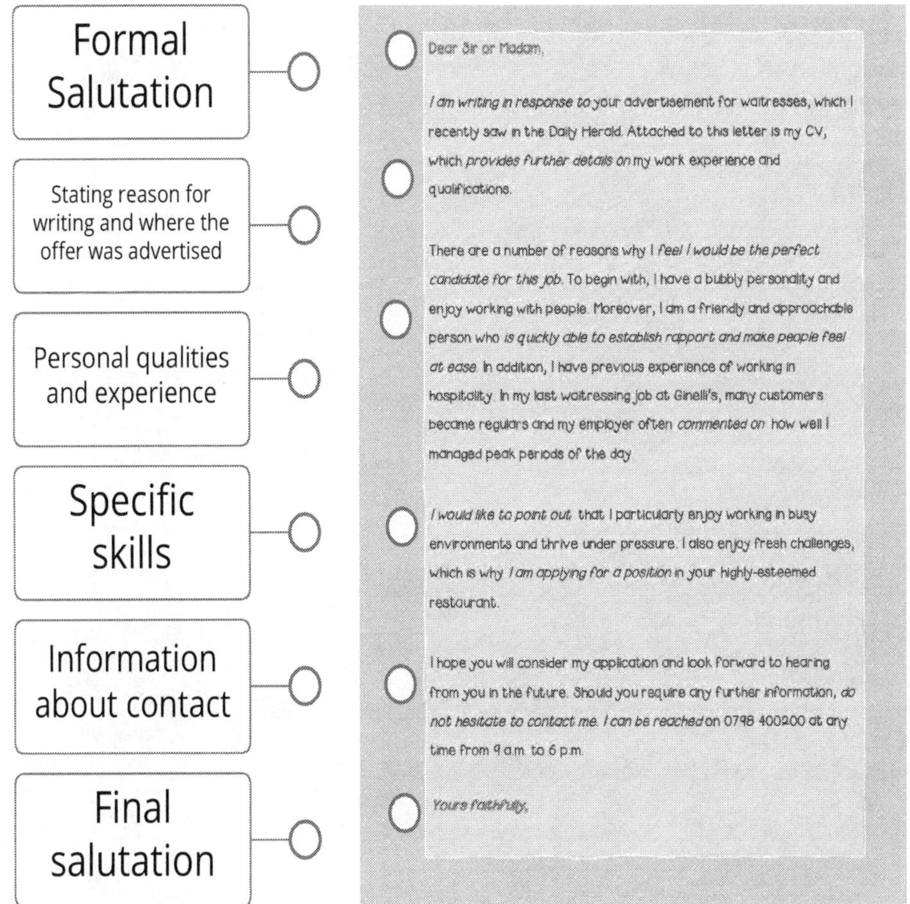

Tailor your application to the specific job, program, or opportunity you are applying for. Carefully review the requirements and expectations outlined in the application, and ensure that your application highlights relevant skills, experiences, and qualifications that align with what they are seeking.

Showcase your accomplishments, experiences, and skills that are relevant to the position or opportunity you are applying for. Provide specific examples and quantify your achievements whenever possible.

Write your application in a clear, concise, and well-organized manner. Use paragraphs to separate different ideas or sections, and ensure that your thoughts flow logically. Avoid using jargon or overly complex language. Keep paragraphs short - **maximum 3 sentences**.

Convey your enthusiasm and genuine interest in the opportunity you are applying for. Explain why you are interested in the position or programme and how it aligns with your long-term goals or aspirations. Share specific reasons or experiences.

If appropriate, include references or recommendation letters.

WRITING A DIARY/JOURNAL

MATCH UP THE IMAGES WITH THE ITEMS YOU MAY WANT TO INCLUDE WHEN WRITING A DIARY ENTRY. TAKE A GUESS IF YOU DON'T KNOW - THEN CHECK THE ANSWERS.

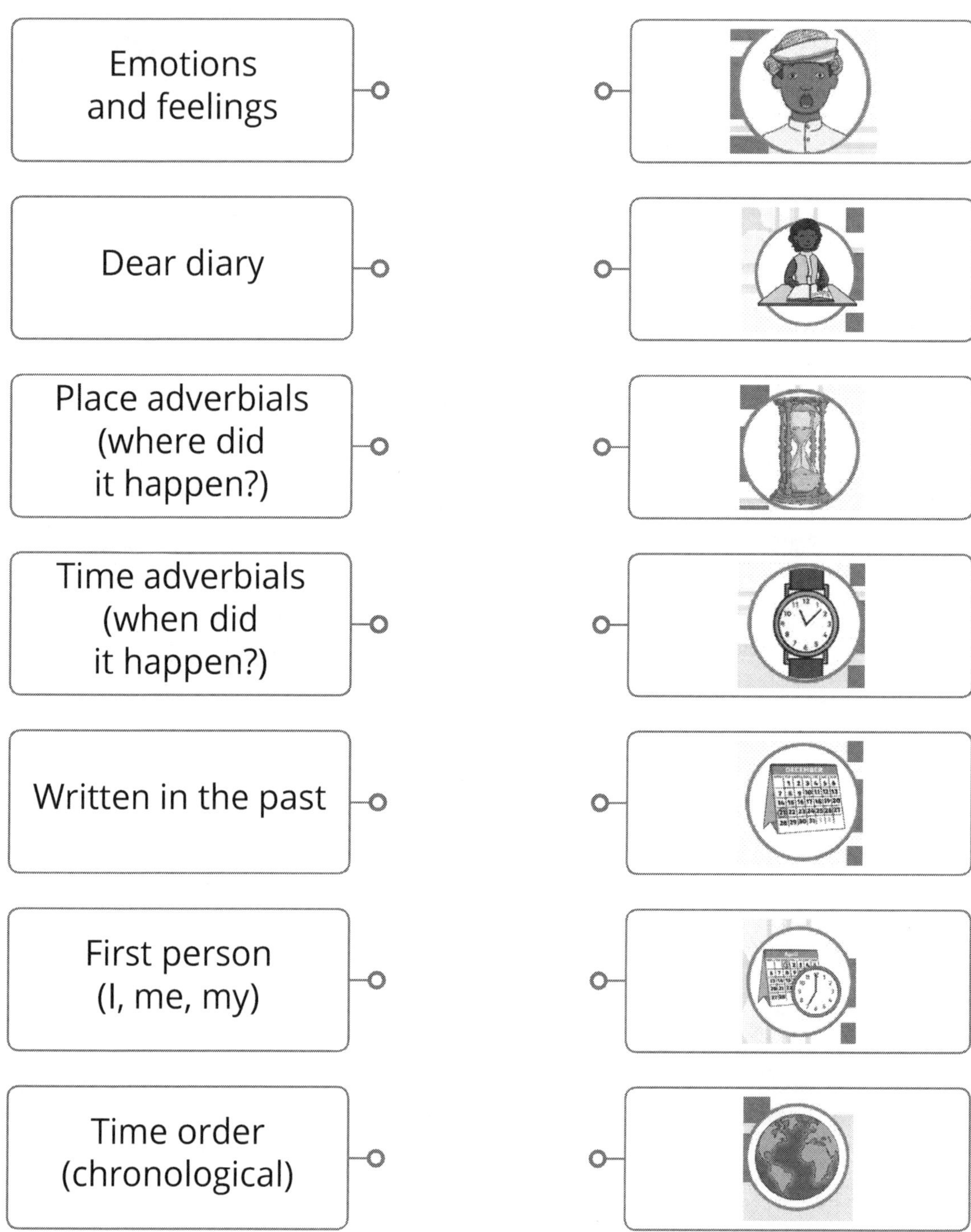

WRITING A BLOG POST

TIPS FOR WRITING A GOOD BLOG/POST - BUT WHERE DO THEY GO?

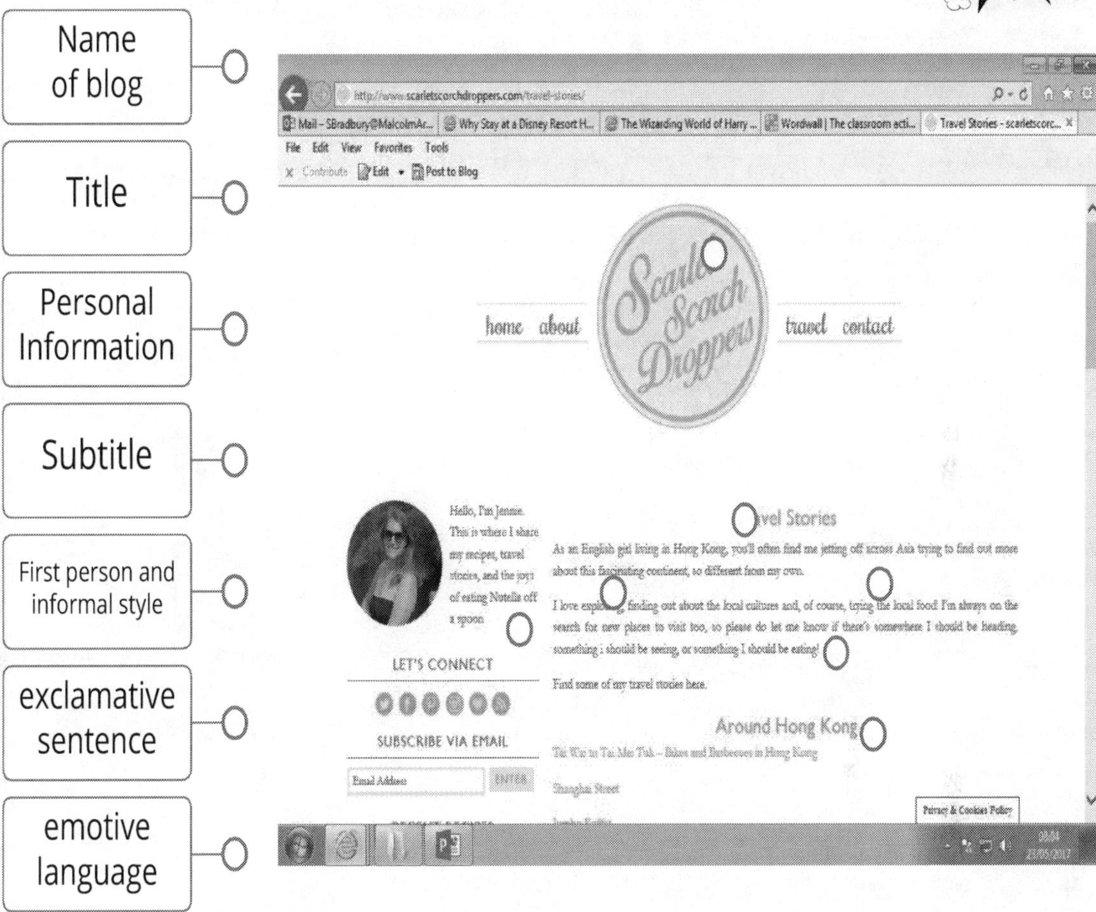

Determine a specific niche or topic for your blog that aligns with your interests, expertise, and target audience.

Create a content strategy that outlines the topics, subtopics, and key themes you want to cover in your blog.

Utilize categories and tags to organize your blog posts. Categories are broad topics that encompass multiple related posts, while tags are specific keywords that describe content.

Design a clear and intuitive navigation menu that makes it easy for visitors to explore your blog and find the information they're looking for.

Break up your blog posts with headings and subheadings to improve readability and organization. Use header tags (H1, H2, H3, etc.) to structure your headings in order of importance.

One of the ways writers create a scene in your mind is by using language features (language techniques) to describe or draw comparisons to other things in normal life that you can picture, or by playing with words and sounds to conjure up feelings. Let's have a look at some of the most common, and easier-to-use examples that you might begin to employ in your writing. If you can use master Language Features it will greatly improve your speaking and writing ability.

Rhetorical Question: Asking a question that does not require a direct answer; it is asked just to make people think, to stimulate the conversation.

Example1: "What time do you call this?!"
Example 2: "Do you really want the people in Africa to starve?"

Using a rhetorical question at the start, or at the very end of a text can be a very powerful tool.

Simile: A comparison between two different things using "like" or "as".

Example 1: "Her hair was as black as coal." (The color of her hair is compared to coal using "as".)
Example 2: "He runs like a cheetah chasing its prey." (The way he runs is compared to a cheetah using "like".)

Metaphor: A comparison between two different things without using "like" or "as" where you are saying something IS something else it cannot be.

Example 1: "Life is a journey." (Life is compared to a journey, implying that both have ups and downs, twists and turns.)
Example 2: "The world is a stage." (The world is compared to a stage, implying that people play different roles in life.)

Personification: Giving human characteristics to non-human things.

Example 1: "The wind whispered through the trees." (The wind is given the human characteristic of whispering.)
Example 2: "The sun smiled down on us." (The sun is given the human characteristic of smiling.)

Hyperbole: An exaggeration used to over emphasise a point.

Example 1: "I've told you a million times!" (The number of times the speaker has repeated themselves is exaggerated for emphasis.)
Exampe 2: "She was so hungry, she could have eaten a horse." (The level of hunger is exaggerated to emphasize how hungry she was.)

Alliteration: The repetition of the same sound at the beginning of words.

Example 1: "Peter Piper picked a peck of pickled peppers." (The "p" sound is repeated throughout the sentence.)
Example 2: "She sells seashells by the seashore." (The "s" sound is repeated throughout the sentence.)

Onomatopoeia: Words that imitate the sound they describe.

Example 1: "The clock tick-tocked in the silent room." (The word "tick-tocked" imitates the sound of a clock.)
Example 2: "The thunder roared in the distance." (The word "roared" imitates the sound of thunder.)

Irony: A contrast between what is expected and what actually happens.

Example 1: "A fire station burns down." (The place that is meant to prevent fires actually catches fire.)
Example 2: "The traffic jam clears up just as you arrive at your destination." (The traffic jam causes the speaker to be delayed, but it clears up as soon as they arrive.)

Symbolism: The use of an object or image to represent an idea or concept.

Example 1: The American flag represents freedom and democracy. (The flag represents larger concepts than just cloth and colors.)
Example 2: The dove is a symbol of peace. (The bird represents a larger concept of peace.)

Repetition: The repeating of a word or phrase for emphasis.

Example 1: "I have a dream that one day this nation will rise up and live out the true meaning of its creed." (The phrase "I have a dream" is repeated for emphasis.)

Example 2: "We shall fight on the beaches, we shall fight on the landing grounds, we shall fight in the fields and in the streets."(The phrase "we shall fight" is repeated for emphasis.)

Rule of Three: Where three words or phrases within the same group can be used together. (Our brain likes to remember things in groups of three).

Example 1: Hands, Face, Space
Example 2: Stop, Look and Listen

Idiom: A saying that in and of itself makes no sense, yet we know what it means.

Example 1: It's raining cats and dogs
Example 2: The ball is in your court

Here's a quick quiz to see if you remember some of the literary features/techniques we have covered. These are just a few. When you have mastered them, look up more examples of literary techniques or language features, such as using humor. We've made this quiz easy - by giving you the answers underneath each question, but try to see how well you do - without looking.

What is a simile?

a) A comparison between two different things without using "like" or "as"
b) A comparison between two different things using "like" or "as"
c) Giving human characteristics to non-human things

Answer: b) A comparison between two different things using "like" or "as"

What is a metaphor?

a) A comparison between two different things without using "like" or "as"
b) A comparison between two different things using "like" or "as"
c) Giving human characteristics to non-human things

Answer: a) A comparison between two different things without using "like" or "as"

What is personification?

a) A comparison between two different things without using "like" or "as"
b) A comparison between two different things using "like" or "as"
c) Giving human characteristics to non-human things

Answer: c) Giving human characteristics to non-human things

What is hyperbole?

a) The repetition of the same sound at the beginning of words
b) The repetition of vowel sounds within words
c) An exaggeration used to emphasize a point

Answer: c) An exaggeration used to emphasize a point

What is alliteration?

a) The repetition of the same sound at the beginning of words
b) The repetition of vowel sounds within words
c) Words that imitate the sound they describe

Answer: a) The repetition of the same sound (not always the same letter) at the beginning of words

What is onomatopoeia?

a) The repetition of the same sound at the beginning of words
b) The repetition of vowel sounds within words
c) Words that imitate the sound they describe

Answer: c) Words that imitate the sound they describe

What is irony?
a) Giving human characteristics to non-human things
b) An exaggeration used to emphasize a point
c) A contrast between what is expected and what actually happens

Answer: c) A contrast between what is expected and what actually happens

What is symbolism?
a) A comparison between two different things without using "like" or "as"
b) Descriptive language that appeals to the senses
c) The use of an object or image to represent an idea or concept

Answer: c) The use of an object or image to represent an idea or concept

What is repetition?
a) Giving a hint or suggestion of what is to come later in the story
b) The repeating of a word or phrase for emphasis
c) A scene that interrupts the narrative to show an event that happened earlier in time

Answer: b) The repeating of a word or phrase for emphasis

What is the Rule of Three?
a) Three separate people mentioned within a paragraph
b) Using three related words to make your point
c) Using three metaphors in one paragraph

Answer: b) Using three related words to make your point

What is tone?
a) The attitude or mood conveyed by the author's writing
b) A comparison between two different things without using "like" or "as"
c) Giving human characteristics to non-human things

Answer: a) The attitude or mood conveyed by the author's writing

What literary technique is used in the sentence "The wind whispered through the trees"?
a) Simile
b) Metaphor
c) Personification

Answer: c) Personification

What literary technique is used in the sentence "Her eyes were like the stars in the sky"?
a) Simile
b) Metaphor
c) Personification

Answer: a) Simile

What literary technique is used in the sentence "My father was a rock in my life"?
a) Simile
b) Metaphor
c) Personification

Answer: c) Metaphor

What literary technique is used in the sentence "The sun smiled down on us"?
a) Simile
b) Metaphor
c) Personification

Answer: c) Personification

What literary technique is used in the sentence "The thunder roared like a lion"?
a) Simile
b) Metaphor
c) Personification

Answer: a) Simile

As you can imagine, using these language tricks to create a picture, describe a feeling or a character, or even create an emotional response in your reader, can be powerful.

Mastering Language Techniques or Langauge Features will bring your writing to life. This is used all the time in long-form writing, where a reader invites you to share a deeper engagement, giving you time to set a scene, and to introduce and develop characters.

Some of the most often used Language Features are:

Direct Address: "**You** do this, **you** should do that."

First Person: "**I** did this, **I** did that."

Simile: "She walked **like** a duck.

Metaphor: "He **was** her **rock**." "The runner **is** lightening quick."

Personification "The **wind whistled** round the tree."

Level 2 Language Features Crossword

Across

2. Using an exaggeration (9)
3. A question that doesn't need an answer (10)
4. A saying that doesn't make sense (5)
8. Opinions or statements which are not neutral (4)
9. Writing intended to be funny (6)
12. Language that makes you feel something (7)
14. Giving an object personal or human traits (15)

Down

1. Using the same word or phrase again (10)
5. Something is 'as' or 'like' something else (6)
6. Something is described as being something else (8)
7. A phrase using the same sounds or letters (12)
10. Words that sound like their meaning... "biff, bash" (11)
11. The writer speaks to you personally (6,7)
13. Using three words or phrases with the same theme together (4,2,5)

LANGUAGE FEATURES QUIZ 1

WORK OUT THE ANSWERS AND THEN FIND THEM IN THE PUZZLE.

1. I've told you a thousand times!
2. What time do you call this?
3. Reuse, Reduce, Recycle
4. Over the moon
5. Her eyes were like diamonds
6. The world is a stage
7. Your country needs YOU!
8. Peter Piper picked a pepper
9. BANG CRASH WALLOP
10. The vine wrapped its arms around the house
11. 100 percent of people will die

LANGUAGE FEATURES - JUMBLED IDIOMS

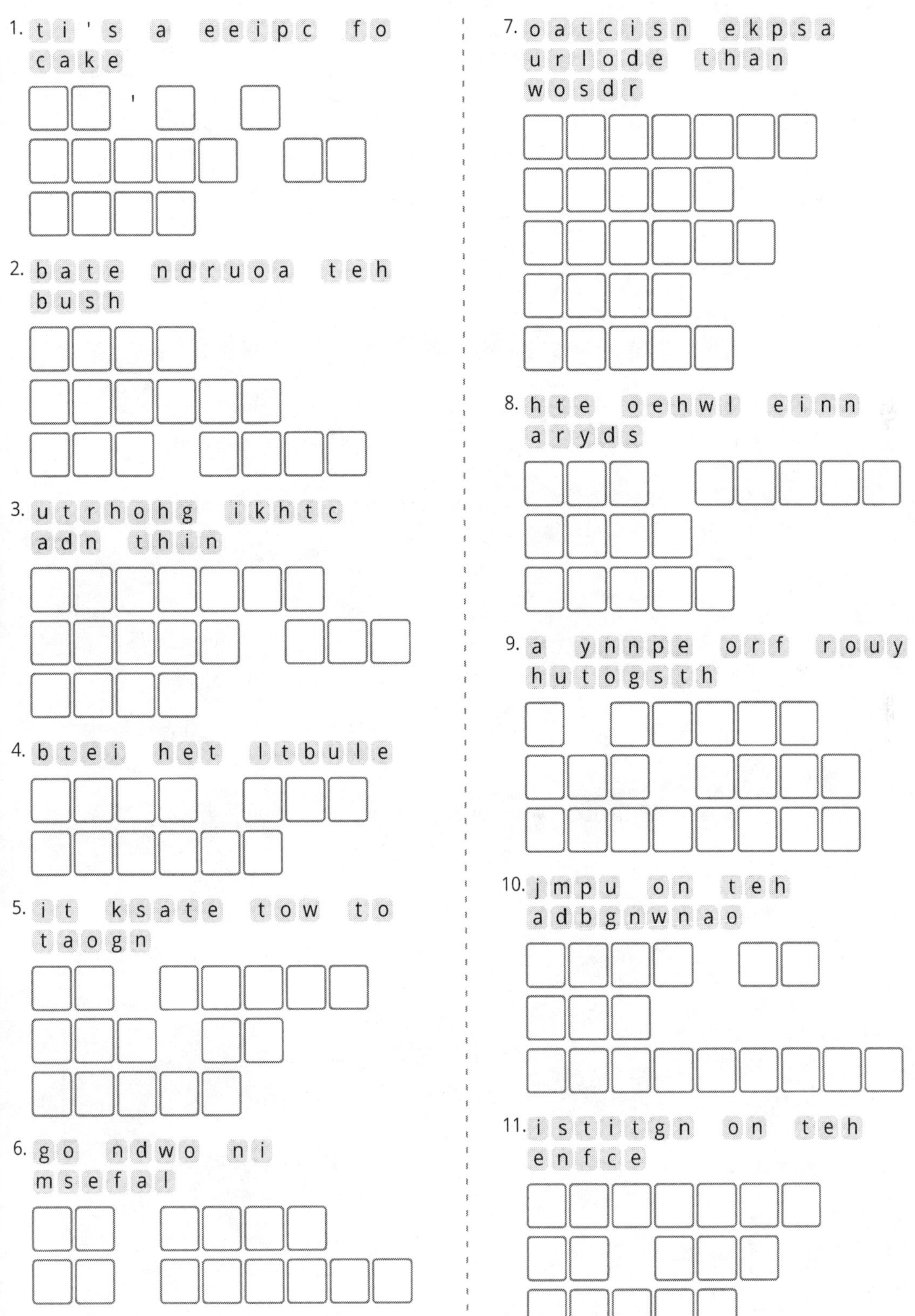

LANGUAGE FEATURES - RHETORICAL QUESTION?

1. What time do you call this?

   A ☐ Rhetorical question B ☐ Not rhetorical question

2. What did you eat for lunch today?

   A ☐ Rhetorical question B ☐ Not rhetorical question

3. Going to bed late will leave you feeling tired in the morning. Who knew?

   A ☐ Rhetorical question B ☐ Not rhetorical question

4. Who is your favourite football player?

   A ☐ Rhetorical question B ☐ Not rhetorical question

5. Every year, millions of trees are cut down and many animals loose their homes. Would you like it if your home was cut down?

   A ☐ Rhetorical question B ☐ Not rhetorical question

6. Cheetahs are 3 times faster than the average human. How amazing is that?

   A ☐ Rhetorical question B ☐ Not rhetorical question

7. What are you doing next weekend?

   A ☐ Rhetorical question B ☐ Not rhetorical question

8. Isn't life wonderful?

   A ☐ Rhetorical question B ☐ Not rhetorical question

9. What did you eat for breakfast?

   A ☐ Rhetorical question B ☐ Not a rhetorical question

LANGUAGE FEATURES - OXYMORON

AN OXYMORON IS WHERE TWO OPPOSITE WORDS GO TOGETHER TO MAKE ONE NEW WORD THAT ACTUALLY MAKES SENSE. AN EXAMPLE MIGHT BE THE WORDS DEAD AND GOOD. ALONE THEY SEEM TO HAVE DIFFERENT MEANINGS. HOW CAN SOMETHING THAT IS DEAD ALSO BE GOOD? BUT WHEN YOU PUT THEM TOGETHER 'DEAD GOOD' MEANS REALLY GOOD. SEE IF YOU CAN MATCH THESE SEEMINGLY OPPOSITE WORDS TO MAKE NEW PHRASES..

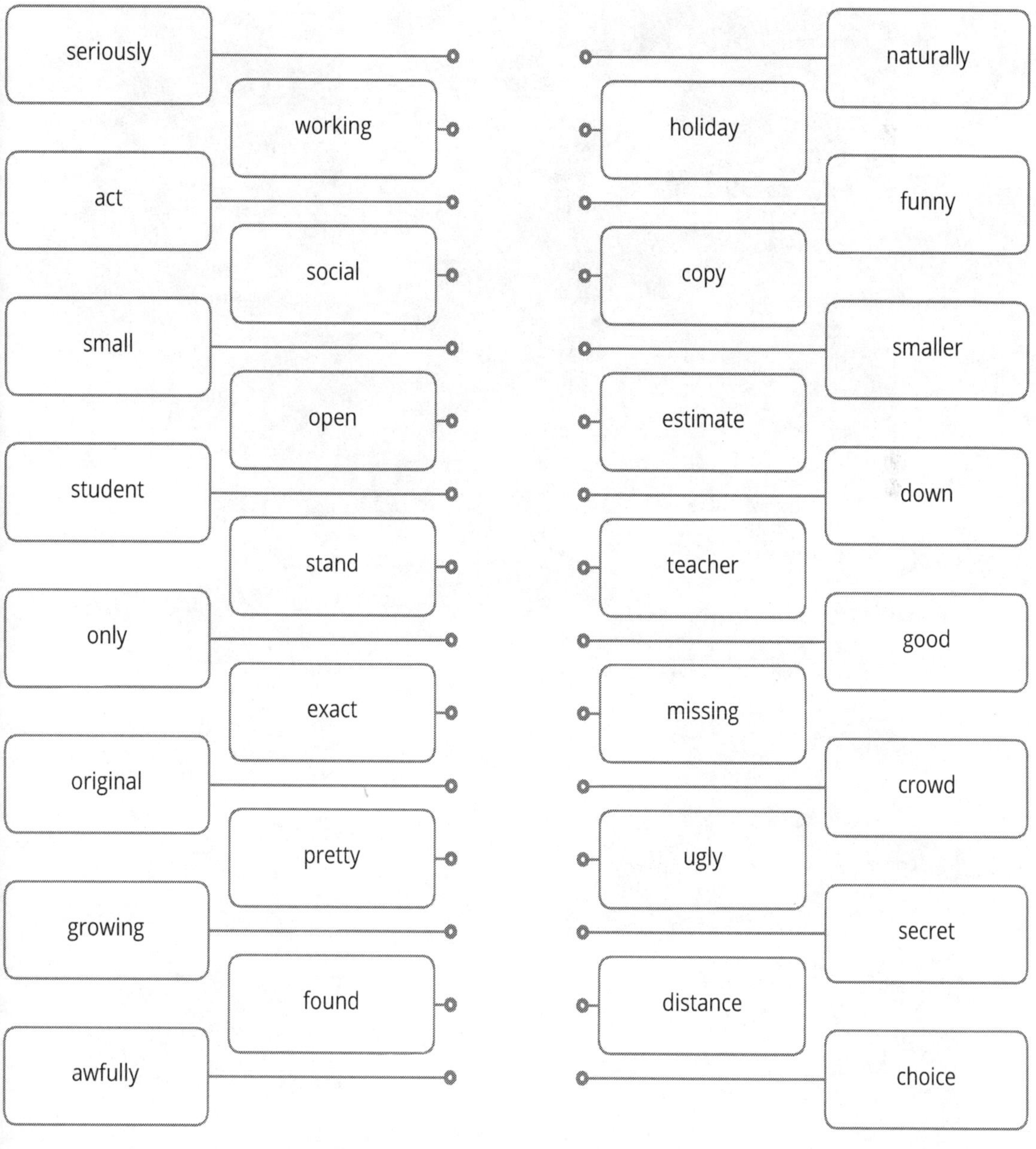

LANGUAGE FEATURES - HYPERBOLE?

1. It was so cold, I saw penguins wearing hats!

A ☐ Hyperbole

B ☐ Not Hyperbole

2. The film was so bad, I thought I would die of boredom!

A ☐ Hyperbole B ☐ Not Hyperbole

3. I like to drink coffee in the morning.

A ☐ Hyperbole B ☐ Not Hyperbole

4. It's so hot, you can fry an egg on the pavement.

A ☐ Hyperbole B ☐ Not Hyperbole

5. The bus is often late.

A ☐ Hyperbole

B ☐ Not Hyperbole

6. I think I've eaten my own body weight in chocolate!

A ☐ Hyperbole

B ☐ Not Hyperbole

7. I'm so tired I could sleep for a week.

A ☐ Hyperbole B ☐ Not Hyperbole

8. He always wears a coat when it's cold.

A ☐ Hyperbole

B ☐ Not Hyperbole

9. She ran like the wind.

A ☐ Hyperbole B ☐ Not Hyperbole

10. My leg hurts.

A ☐ Hyperbole B ☐ Not Hyperbole

LANGUAGE FEATURES - SIMILE/METAPHOR?

Write in the item numbers in the list of boxes for each group

Similes ☐☐☐☐☐☐☐☐☐☐

Metaphors ☐☐☐☐☐☐☐☐☐☐

1. I'm a night owl.
2. Della is as strong as an ox.
3. Baby, you're a firework.
4. Trouble is a friend of mine.
5. That was as easy as shooting fish in a barrel.
6. My brother and sister fight like cats and dogs.
7.  Karen ran like the wind.
8.  He rules with an iron fist.
9.  That film was like watching paint dry.
10.  Let's get all our ducks in a row.
11.  Veronica sings like an angel.
12. My room is as clean as a whistle.
13. You're as cold as ice.
14.  He is as brave as a lion.
15.  Emma was the black sheep of the family.
16.  Bob has a heart of gold.
17. It's raining cats and dogs.
18.  Dylan is a ray of light.
19.  You ain't nothin' but a hound dog.
20.  Shelly was as quiet as a mouse.

LANGUAGE FEATURES - CROSSWORD

Across

2. repetition of words starting with same letter (12)
3. stating something that's objective (5)
4. stating something that's subjective (8)
5. questions that don't require answer (10,9)
8. using numbers, percentages etc (10)
10. short story to illustrate point (8)
11. making audience laugh or smile (6)
13. reporting wise or respected words (10)
14. exaggerating for effect (9)

Down

1. speaking to the audience "you" (6,7)
6. stating something more than once for effect (10)
7. Language that appeals to emotions (pathos) (7,8)
9. List of three for effect (4,2,5)
12. call for action (6)

LANGUAGE FEATURES - SIMILE/METAPHOR?

PUT A TICK UNDER EACH MOLE WHO HAS A SIMILE

You probably speak informally, most of us do. You use simple sentences made up of simple words, and you get to the point as quickly as possible. You very rarely come across someone who talks to you in a very formal way, using elongated words and complex sentences that are sometimes difficult to understand. Life would be hard for us all if we had to concentrate on every single word to try to find meaning in someone's speech. Life is too short.

But, on the other hand, in a world of 'text speak' abbreviated words can often leave the uninitiated confused. The younger age groups - including probably yourself, have 'text speak' down to an art, and it behooves older folk to get on board or they will be left in the dark - not having a clue what their younger counterparts are saying. So, there are several forms of informal language - the way most of us speak, slang, text speak and language based on culture. The words and abbreviations often used in texts are similar to ones used in conversation by older generations - but may have vastly different meanings.

These abbreviations, to fit the limited number of characters allowed on some messaging services, are probably very familiar. But be aware that many people do not have a clue what they mean:

10Q - Thank you
2M2H - Too much to handle
AAS - Alive and smiling
AQAP - As quickly as possible
DBBSWF - Dream boat body, Shipwreck face
MUAH - Multiple unsuccessful attempts at humour
PLOS -Parents looking over the shoulder

In some forms of communication, formal writing is essential. For most business situations, letters and legal documents are often written very formally. Think of contracts, to rent an apartment, or even to sign up with a mobile carrier, or a movie streaming service; they are mostly written formally. This is because they are legal documents, and anytime it's legal, there's a whole lot of verbiage that needs to be included, much of which we 'regular people' don't understand.

You will be required on many occasions - surprisingly many occasions - to write formally. You might have to write to a college enquiring about a course of study, a council to complain, apply for a job, to include a cover letter when returning a product. Yes, in a world where we think 'no one writes letters anymore' - there are quite a few times when you will have to put pen to paper, or at least type on a keyboard - a formal piece of written communication. So, you must be able to differentiate between formal and informal writing. Let us commence.(Formal) Here we go! (Informal)

SLANG/Very Informal	INFORMAL/normal	FORMAL
Wanna		
Gonna		
Y'all		
Dude		
Chill		
Awesome		
Laid-back		
Outta		
Kinda		
Bummer		

Formal Text Rules:

- Uses standard grammar rules and vocabulary.
- Avoids contractions (say 'do not', not don't, say 'could not', not couldn't) and slang.
- Uses full sentences and avoids fragments.
- Avoids personal pronouns (e.g. "I", "we", "you") and instead uses third-person pronouns (e.g. "he", "she", "they").
- Follows a specific format or structure, such as in academic papers, legal documents, or business letters.
- Uses more technical or specialized vocabulary.
- Usually written to people we do not know.

Informal Text Rules:

- Uses slang and contractions.
- Uses shorter sentences and sentence fragments.
- Uses personal pronouns (e.g. "I", "we", "you") more freely.
- Includes idiomatic expressions and colloquialisms (local words).
- Can be more conversational in tone.
- Often used in text messages, social media posts, or personal emails.

Level 2 Formal and Informal Letters

Write in the item numbers in the list of boxes for each group

Formal ☐☐☐☐☐☐☐☐☐☐☐☐

Informal ☐☐☐☐☐☐☐☐☐☐☐☐

1. Please find enclosed ...
2. See you soon.
3. Please contact me if you require any further information.
4. Thanks for your letter.
5. I want to know about ...
6. I am writing to apply for the position of ...
7. I would like to confirm that ...
8. Yours sincerely,
9. I look forward to hearing from you.
10. Dear Nanny and Grandad,
11. I am writing to express my concerns.
12. Let me know if it's OK.
13. Hi!
14. To whom it may concern.
15. Give my love to ...
16. I'm writing to tell you that ...
17. Dear Mrs Smith,
18. Yours faithfully,
19. Dear Sir or Madam,
20. Best wishes,
21. With reference to your letter dated ...
22. Lots of love.
23. I got your letter.

Formal v Informal Level 2 Quiz 2

PUT A TICK UNDER THE FORMAL MOLES. NO SLANG, NO TEXT SPEAK.

Formal v Informal Level 2 Quiz 3

Write in the item numbers in the list of boxes for each group

THIS TIME YOU ARE LOOKING FOR THE INFORMAL WORDS FIRST - THEN FORMAL

Correct ☐☐☐☐☐ ☐☐☐☐ — INFORMAL

Incorrect ☐☐☐☐☐ ☐☐☐☐ — FORMAL

1	2	3
ACQUAINTANCE	VEHICLES	GENTLEMEN
4	**5**	**6**
ACE	ENQUIRE	PIDDLY
7	**8**	**9**
MATE	INSIGNIFICANT	DELIGHTED
10	**11**	**12**
WELL HAPPY	GRANNY	CHUFFED
13	**14**	**15**
RATHER SPLENDID	BLOKE	KID
16	**17**	**18**
SPECTACLES	SPECS	BEVERAGE

We live in a world now where facts and opinions seem interchangeable, where it's often difficult to determine fact from fiction, and where previously reliable sources now flaunt infotainment as news, and officials openly present "alternative facts." But, let's be clear that facts and opinions are two distinctly different beasts, and should be handled with care.

- A fact is a statement that can be proven true or false based on objective evidence or data. Facts are verifiable and do not change based on personal beliefs or feelings. For example, "The Earth revolves around the Sun" is a fact that can be proven through scientific evidence.

- An opinion is a personal belief or judgment about a topic or issue. Opinions are subjective and can vary from person to person. They are often based on personal experiences, values, or beliefs, and are not necessarily based on objective evidence or data. For example, "Chocolate ice cream is the best flavor" is an opinion, as it is based on personal preference rather than objective evidence.

Generally, you can spot true information if it contains:

STATISTICS
NUMBERS
DATES
EVENTS
HISTORICAL
NON-FICTION

and is said by an authority, such as:

A PROFESSIONAL OR EXPERT IN THAT FIELD
A PROFESSIONAL BODY/ORGANIZATION
A SCHOOL, UNIVERSITY, OR OTHER EDUCATIONAL FACILITY
RESEARCH BODY
AN OFFICIAL REPORT

But, be aware that even professionals, speaking about an area they know a lot about - STILL HAVE AN OPINION. Be careful to differentiate between the factual information they may have to share, from their own opinion on the matter. Remember, almost everyone has some kind of agenda, some form of bias, whether openly or hidden and that they may not even be aware they are pushing that agenda or opinion.

You really need to be a full-on detective, looking for clues to pick out the fact from the fiction, or fact from opinion. The golden rule to ask yourself when reading, or writing a text is:

Can this information be proven?

There are other clues you can look for. The use of ADJECTIVES (describing words) is an absolute giveaway clue. Fact is not usually associated with lots of adjectives like:

Wonderful, Great, Best, Biggest, Smallest, Nicest... in fact, any word that ends in ...est is a clue that this piece of writing is an opinion. In addition to EST endings, also look for ER at the end - such as Bigger, Better, Greater, etc. These are opinion words.

"The new Jaguar XJS model is the fastEST car on the road!" It may well be a fast car, but unless this statement is followed up by some statistics that compare it to every other fast car currently available and considered a road car, then the statement is opinion.

Opinions can be easily recognised when they use words like:
THINK, BELIEVE, SUGGEST, PERHAPS, PROBABLY, USUALLY, TYPICALLY, SHOULD, and MUST. Opinions also use judgement words such as: GOOD, BAD, BEST, WORST, MOST, LEAST, TERRIBLE, FANTASTIC and AWFUL.

FUN

ALL JUST OPINIONS

Bigger - Better - Stronger
Best - Greatest - Widest - Longest
Kindest - Nicest - Gentlest

"I believe that..."
"I think that..."

"It will change your life...."
"There's never been another one like it..."

Marvelous - Wonderful - Fantastic
Amazing - Brilliant - Awesome

Level 2 Fact or Opinion? Flying

Draw a path from each airplane to its answer - don't crash into other clouds along the way

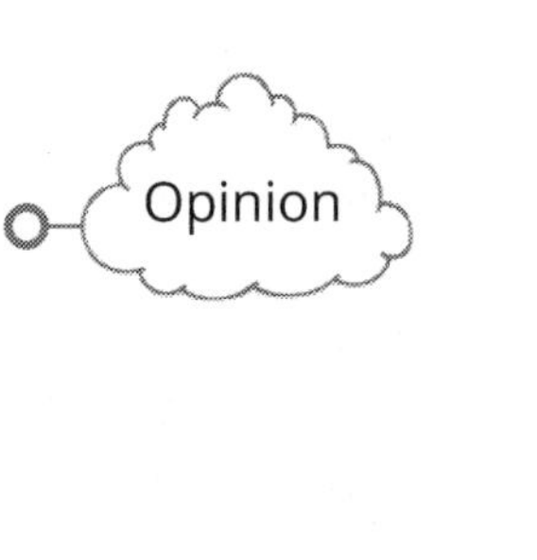

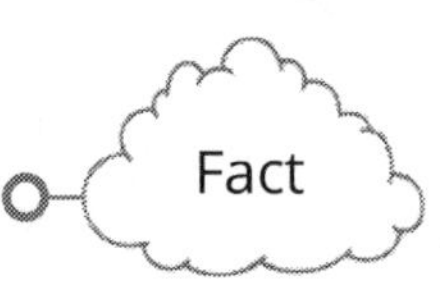

AND, HERE'S A SURPRISE YOU MAY FIND DIFFICULT TO ACCEPT ABOUT OPINION. EVEN IF SOMEONE YOU REALLY TRUST GIVES YOU A NEW PIECE OF INFORMATION - IT DOESN'T MAKE IT TRUE!

YOUR LOVED ONES ARE NOT THE AUTHORITY ON TRUTH. THEY ONLY SHARE WHAT THEY BELIEVE TO BE TRUE, BUT IF IT CANNOT BE PROVEN - THEN IT IS ONLY THEIR OPINION. TRUTH IS ALWAYS VERIFIABLE; CAN BE PROVEN.

- CHALLENGE AND VERIFY EVERYTHING YOU READ ONLINE.

Level 2 Fact or Opinion

DRAW A LINE FROM THE STATEMENTS TO THE RIGHT ANSWER - FACT OR OPINION. HOW GOOD ARE YOU AT TELLING THE DIFFERENCE?

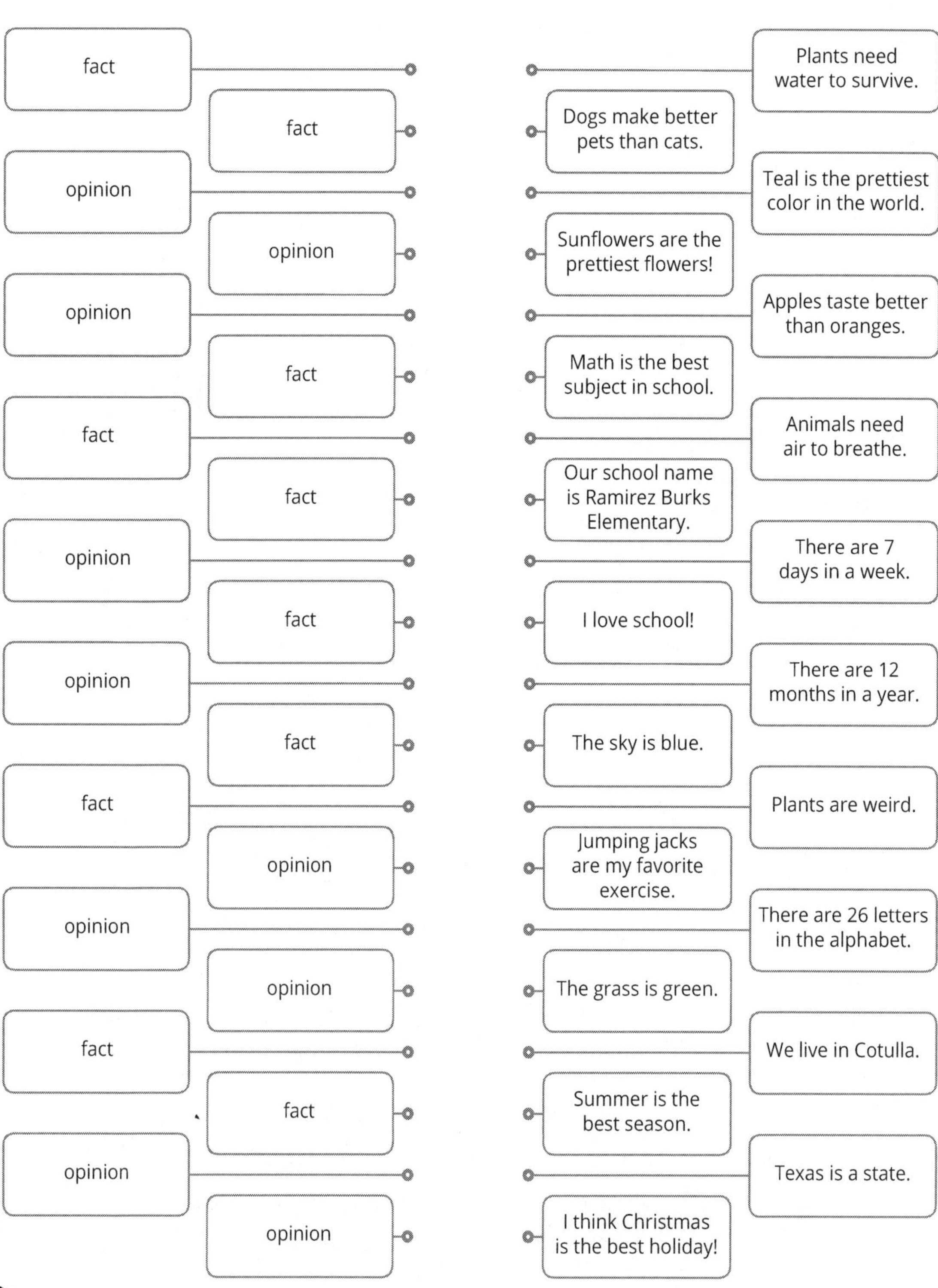

Level 2 Fact v Opinion Quiz 1

1. The sky is blue (sometimes).

   A ☐ fact B ☐ opinion

2. Purple is the prettiest colour in the world.

   A ☐ fact B ☐ opinion

3. The grass is green in the Winter.

   A ☐ fact B ☐ opinion

4. Apples taste better than oranges.

   A ☐ opinion B ☐ fact

5. Dogs make better pets than cats.

   A ☐ fact B ☐ opinion

6. California is better than Florida.

   A ☐ opinion B ☐ fact

7. London is great.

   A ☐ fact B ☐ opinion

8. London is a large city.

   A ☐ fact B ☐ opinion

9. Tea is much nicer than coffee.

   A ☐ fact B ☐ opinion

10. There are 26 letters in the alphabet.

    A ☐ fact B ☐ opinion

11. Summer is the best season.

    A ☐ fact B ☐ opinion

12. English is the best subject in college!

    A ☐ opinion B ☐ fact

13. The flight from London to New York is shorter than flying from London to Los Angeles.

    A ☐ opinion B ☐ fact

14. There are 7 days in a week.

    A ☐ fact B ☐ opinion

15. Plants need water to survive.

    A ☐ fact B ☐ opinion

16. Sunflowers are the prettiest flowers!

    A ☐ fact B ☐ opinion

17. Jumping jacks are the best exercise.

    A ☐ opinion B ☐ fact

18. There are 12 months in a year.

    A ☐ opinion B ☐ fact

19. Plants are weird.

    A ☐ opinion B ☐ fact

20. Animals need air to breathe.

    A ☐ opinion B ☐ fact

Level 2 Fact vs Opinion Quiz 2

NOW

Write in the item numbers in the list of boxes for each group

Fact

Opinion

1. School uniforms are a great idea
2. Exercise is good for you
3. Toast is better than Crumpets
4. Paris is the capital city of France
5. Monopoly is a board game
6. Monopoly is a great board game
7. Bran Flakes are the perfect breakfast
8. Eating vegetables is good for you
9. You should get a haircut
10. Some farmers in Lincolnshire grow vegetables
11. People in Manchester are friendlier than those in London
12. Charles III is the King of England
13. Kids on computers is never good
14. Some schools make their pupils wear uniforms
15. New York is a city
16. Money brings happiness
17. The Battle of Hastings was in 1066
18. Carrots are better than sprouts
19. Golden Delicious and Granny Smith are apples
20. Eating breakfast is good for you
21. Trainers are more comfortable than shoes
22. All children should play Cricket
23. Cricket is a fantastic sport
24. Parrots are the most intelligent birds
25. Joe Biden was the 46th President of the USA
26. All children should wear school uniforms

HOME

If you are ever asked to give a talk or a presentation - as you are in school or college, a great way to outline your talk or presentation is to use a mind map as shown below.

Each circle can represent a powerpoint/google slide in your presentation. You can simply put a few prompt words on each slide. Do not put the exact words you are going to speak on the slide. There should be a maximum of six words on each slide - so say the experts. But, you can just put one or two words - the words from your mind map. Use these as prompts. Can you speak for 1 to 2 minutes on each of these subjects in the circles? If so, your talk is complete! Remember to sum up at the end, and then invite questions.

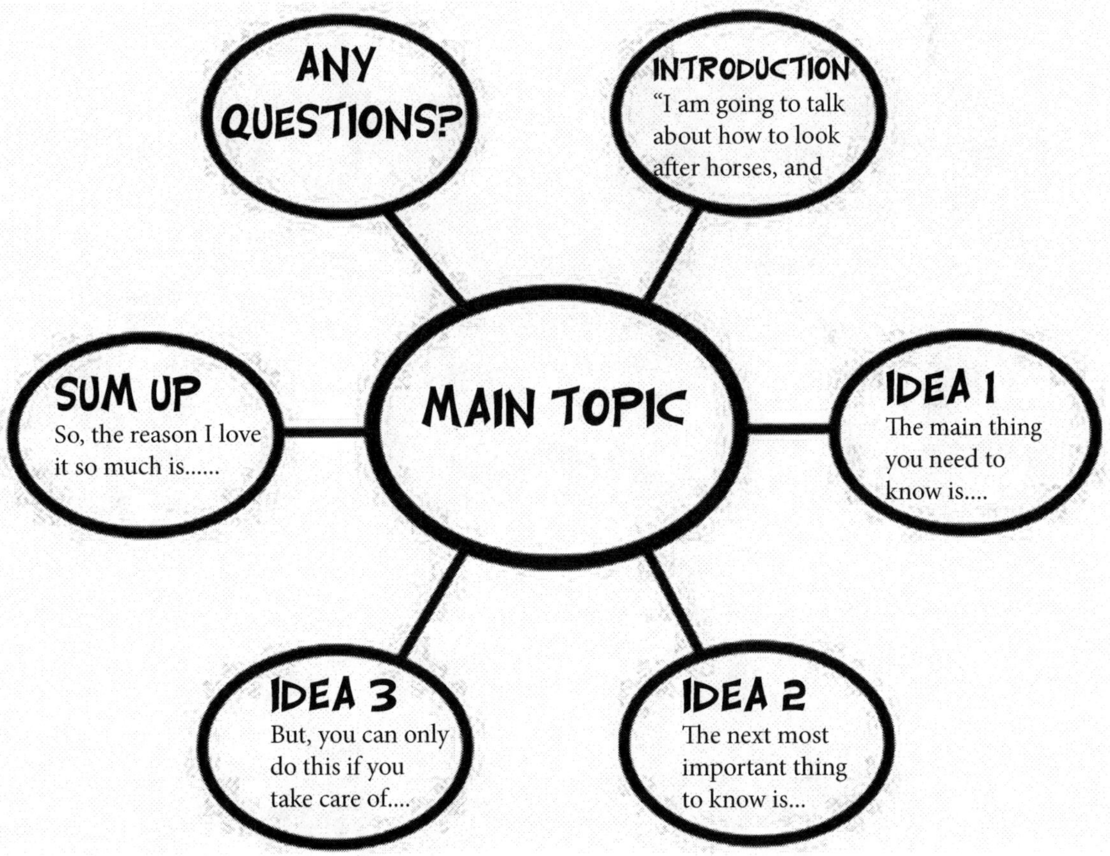

ANY QUESTIONS?

INTRODUCTION
"I am going to talk about how to look after horses, and

SUM UP
So, the reason I love it so much is......

MAIN TOPIC

IDEA 1
The main thing you need to know is....

IDEA 3
But, you can only do this if you take care of....

IDEA 2
The next most important thing to know is...

You could place the mind map on a table in front of you to refer to. But, if you have these words on the slides, then you will not need to look down. Just glance at the next slide, and keep looking and smiling at the audience. Again, practice talking for 1 - 2 minutes on each of the circle titles - and that will give you a good 8 minute talk. If you are only required to do 5 minutes in total, then just speak for one minute on each circle or slide title.

YOU'VE GOT THIS!

Write in the item numbers in the list of boxes for each group

SOME TIPS FOR GIVING A GOOD PRESENTATION - BUT DO YOU KNOW WHICH ARE GOOD TO USE, AND WHICH YOU SHOULD STAY CLEAR OF DOING?

DO this! ☐ ☐ ☐ ☐ ☐

DON'T do this! ☐ ☐ ☐ ☐ ☐

1. Look very serious
2. Try to smile
3. Introduce yourself
4. Be interrupted by your phone
5. Say the topic or aim of your presentation
6. Talk quickly - you need to say a lot in a little time
7. Finish by summing up
8. Make eye contact / look at the camera
9. Read aloud from a script
10. Speak quietly

THERE IS NO WAY FOR US TO GIVE YOU EVERY WORD YOU NEED TO KNOW BY NOW IN LIFE - BUT IF YOU CAN LEARN TO SPELL THESE WORDS - THEY ARE EACH AN EXAMPLE OF OTHER SIMILARLY SPELT WORDS - SO THESE WILL GIVE YOU A GOOD START.

accessible	accidentally	acquaint	acquire	advertisement	annual
appearance	arrangement	awkward	beautiful	because	believe
benefitted	calendar	choose			
ceiling	committee	comparative	conscience	conscientious	conscious
criticism	deceit	defense	description	desirable	desparately
difference	difference	disagreeable	disappear		
dissatisfied	eighth	efficient	embarrassment	excellent	excessive
exciting	excitement	exercise	exhilerating	existence	extraordinary
favorite	fortunately	fortieth			
fulfil	fulfilled	gauge	glamorous	government	harass
height	heir	honorary	humor	immediately	imminent
incidentally	install				
interested	irrelevant	knowledge	liaison	leisure	loose
maintain	maintenance	marvelous	miniature	miscellaneous	mischievous
necessarily	neighbor	ninth			
noticeable	nuisance	occasion	occur	occurrence	occurring
omission	opportunity	panicked	parallel	parliament	particularly
pastime	playwright	possess			
prefer	prejudice	premises	preparation	privilege	proceed
profession	prominent	publicly	pursue	quay	queue
quiet	quite	receipt			
receive	recommend	relevant	schedule	scissors	seize
separate	siege	skilful	stationery	stationary	strength
succeed	surprise	temporary			
tendency	tragedy	twelfth	unneccessary	unparalleled	until
vicious	vigorous	vinegar	waist	waste	wednesday
weird	wired				

THESE ARE SOME OF THE WORDS YOU SHOULD PROBABLY KNOW BY NOW. WE'VE PUT THEM INTO 9 GROUPS TO MAKE IT EASIER TO TEST IN THE QUIZZES OVER THE NEXT FEW PAGES. GOOD LUCK!

Level 2 Spelling Whack a Mole

PUT A TICK UNDER THE MOLES WITH THE CORRECT SPELLING

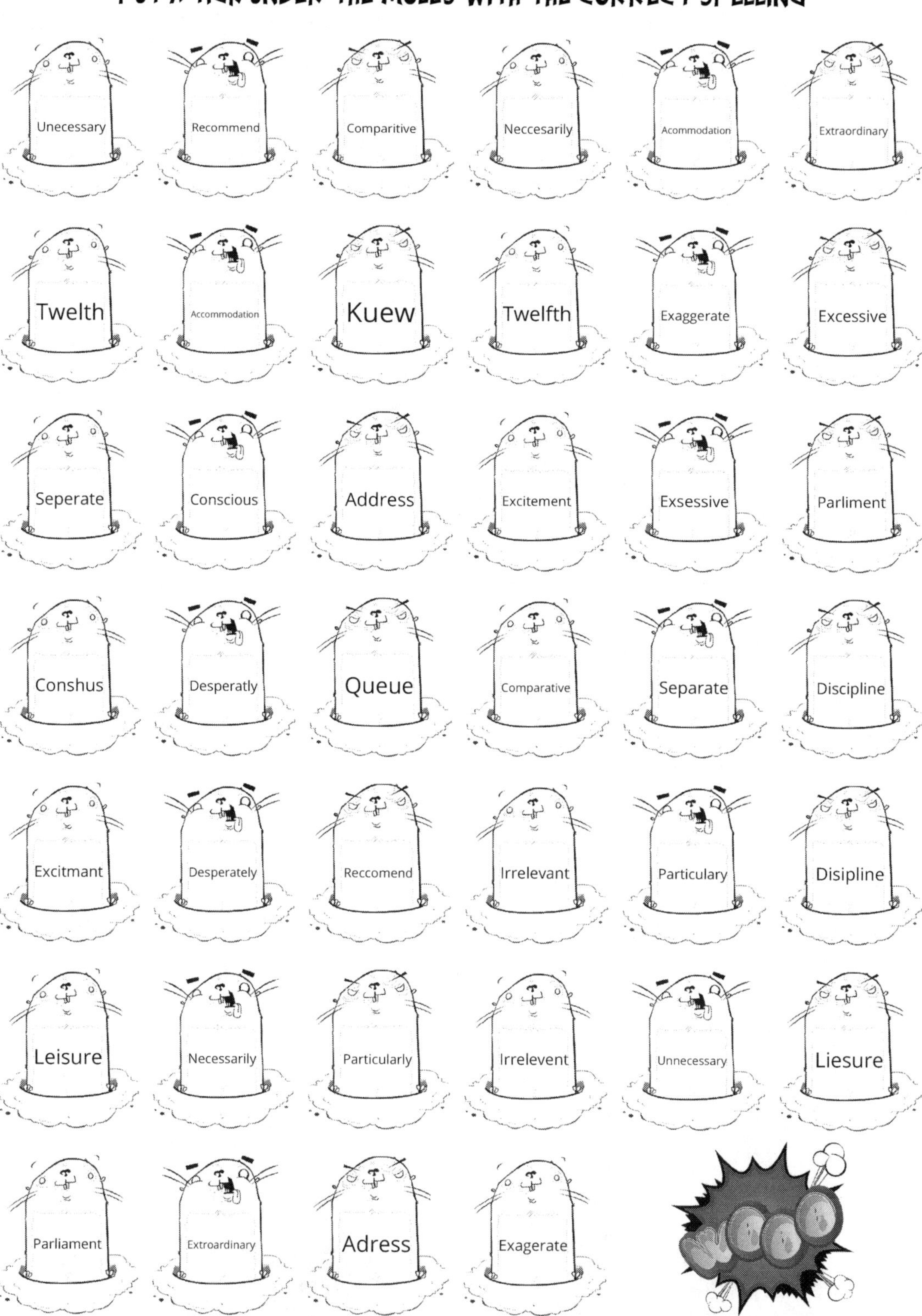

Level 2 How do you spell that? Correct or Incorrect?

1. breathe

A ☐ Correct B ☐ Incorrect

2. appeer

A ☐ Correct B ☐ Incorrect

3. exercise

A ☐ Correct B ☐ Incorrect

4. favorite

A ☐ Correct B ☐ Incorrect

5. bisness

A ☐ Correct B ☐ Incorrect

6. miniture

A ☐ Correct B ☐ Incorrect

7. recommend

A ☐ Correct B ☐ Incorrect

8. eighth

A ☐ Correct B ☐ Incorrect

9. excersize

A ☐ Correct B ☐ Incorrect

10. certun

A ☐ Correct B ☐ Incorrect

11. definate

A ☐ Correct B ☐ Incorrect

12. favourite

A ☐ Correct B ☐ Incorrect

13. separate

A ☐ Correct B ☐ Incorrect

14. breethe

A ☐ Correct B ☐ Incorrect

15. tragedy

A ☐ Correct B ☐ Incorrect

16. build

A ☐ Correct B ☐ Incorrect

17. awkward

A ☐ Correct B ☐ Incorrect

18. aith

A ☐ Correct B ☐ Incorrect

19. breadth

A ☐ Correct B ☐ Incorrect

20. lesure

A ☐ Correct B ☐ Incorrect

21. buetiful

A ☐ Correct B ☐ Incorrect

22. calendar

A ☐ Correct B ☐ Incorrect

23. caught

A ☐ Correct B ☐ Incorrect

24. queue

A ☐ Correct B ☐ Incorrect

25. calander

A ☐ Correct B ☐ Incorrect

26. arkward

A ☐ Correct B ☐ Incorrect

27. believe

A ☐ Correct B ☐ Incorrect

28. beautiful

A ☐ Correct B ☐ Incorrect

Level 2 Spelling Quiz 1

1. accessible	2. accidentally	3. acquaint	4. acquire
5. advertisement	6. annual	7. appearance	8. arrangement
9. awkward	10. beautiful	11. because	12. believe
13. benefitted	14. calendar	~~15. choose~~	

L	S	D	X	W	C	W	F	T	W	Y	U	H	M	L	I
A	R	O	L	W	N	S	I	Y	D	J	V	G	Q	Z	K
N	Q	R	H	W	A	C	Q	U	I	R	E	I	W	B	J
N	M	K	B	E	A	U	T	I	F	U	L	I	M	A	G
U	V	G	S	V	J	A	C	C	E	S	S	I	B	L	E
A	J	Y	A	D	V	E	R	T	I	S	E	M	E	N	T
L	B	E	L	I	E	V	E	C	A	L	E	N	D	A	R
U	A	C	C	I	D	E	N	T	A	L	L	Y	A	P	X
S	C	M	N	L	Y	T	K	A	N	V	R	D	C	F	I
F	D	A	P	P	E	A	R	A	N	C	E	A	Q	J	Y
G	E	B	J	E	L	R	F	M	S	J	T	L	U	J	H
A	W	K	W	A	R	D	Y	S	P	W	R	D	A	X	M
B	E	N	E	F	I	T	T	E	D	Y	Q	W	I	D	U
Q	K	C	C	H	O	O	S	E	Q	K	J	M	N	A	P
G	H	A	R	R	A	N	G	E	M	E	N	T	T	N	O
C	X	B	E	C	A	U	S	E	W	P	Z	F	K	V	G

Level 2 Spelling Quiz 1

NOTICE THAT THE ANAGRAM QUIZ USES THE SAME WORDS AS THE WORDSEARCH

1. s i c l s a b e e c

2. n d i a t y c l c l a e

3. c t i a u n q a

4. i u c a r e q

5. a d i e t s m t e n r e v

6. n a u l n a

7. r a p c a a n e e p

8. r a n e e n a r m t g

9. a w w a r d k

10. u l e i u b t a f

11. u a e b s e c

12. e i e b v e l

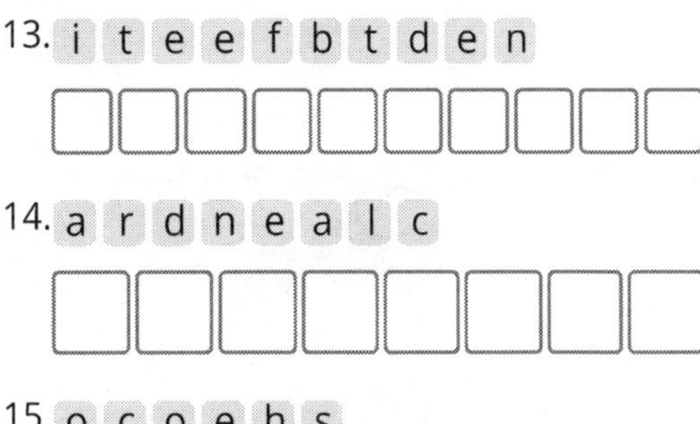

13. i t e e f b t d e n

14. a r d n e a l c

15. o c o e h s

C H O O S E

UNSCRAMBLE THESE WORDS TO SPELL OUT THE WORDS YOU JUST FOUND ON THE LEFT HAND PAGE.

FOR EXAMPLE; YOU FOUND THE WORD CHOOSE IN THE WORD SEARCH. NOW YOU NEED TO FIND THE SCRAMBLED VERSION OF THE WORD CHOOSE HERE.

SPELL IT CORRECTLY IN THE SPACE PROVIDED ON THIS PAGE.

GOT IT?

AS CLEAR AS MUD!

LEVEL 2 SPELLING QUIZ 2

1. ceiling
2. committee
3. comparative
4. conscience
5. conscientious
6. conscious
7. criticism
8. deceit
9. defense
10. description
11. desirable
12. desparately
13. difference
14. disagreeable
15. disappear

Y B T K J M V R C R I T I C I S M
L C O M M I T T E E C D D S E E U
J F O V W Z I Z F W O I I X B D A
F C O N S C I O U S N S S I V E H
F D E S I R A B L E S A A X V S P
Z H K E O W D M Z P C P G Z O P C
R U U P K I P N R L I P R J S A O
V B C E I L I N G S E E E W V R N
A F D T G L Z D J P N A E A O A S
M G S T D V V T P L T R A C X T C
D I F F E R E N C E I K B F S E I
D J A Y U M Y V N U O C L R V L E
E Q W W W N U H E W U S E A F Y N
C Q J Q K N A W O C S V V Q F X C
E C O M P A R A T I V E F J G D E
I Q D E F E N S E P A Q J B R R V
T D D E S C R I P T I O N Y E X B

1. n i e i c l g

2. m i o c e t m e t

3. a t o m e a p v r i c

4. o c e c n i n s e c

5. i t c s u c s n n e o i o

6. s c o c u i n s o

7. t i r c s c i m i

8. d c e t i e

9. s f e n d e e

10. r t e s n p c o i i d

11. i r e d l a s e b

12. a t e s y a p l r e d

13. i e e c n r f f e d

14. g e e r b a i a e d l s

15. a p i d a p s r e

REMEMBER, YOU ARE LOOKING FOR THE SAME WORDS YOU FOUND IN THE WORDSEARCH

LEVEL 2 SPELLING QUIZ 3

1. dissatisfied
2. eighth
3. efficient
4. embarrassment
5. excellent
6. excessive
7. exciting
8. excitement
9. exercise
10. exhilarating
11. existence
12. extraordinary
13. favorite
14. fortunately
15. fortieth

O R N N C E T V N F O R T I E T H
E R J R T F L G O J Q I Y V I D I
M E E H I F Z V V W V R D O E E E
B X X C A I N V P V R A J I E T X
A H C E V C N O I K J G F S T F T
R I I X H I Z R S C N S I O V O R
R L T C Y E J X K I I C K D S R A
A A E E P N X O T T R X T M I T O
S R M S E T L I A E V G Z O D U R
S A E S F E C S X E Y M M I M N D
M T N I R X S E X U I U P Z M A I
E I T V E I Z E W J H G O D G T N
N N T E D B M R Q E G W H H D E A
T G E X C E L L E N T C C T A L R
M B D I W G J U Y N F N D O H Y Y
U Y F A V O R I T E U N K H D S O
U X O Y E U R U E X I S T E N C E

1. s s t i d i s a d f e i

2. e h i h t g

3. f e i i c n f e t

4. e t b s a r n r s m m a e

5. c e l e l n x e t

6. c i s e s v x e e

7. t n c i i e g x

8. i e n t c e t x m e

9. c s e i r e e x

10. i a a x e i h l g t n r

11. i n e s t c x e e

12. e y t i r o r a d x n r a

13. r t v i o f e a

14. t l y r t e n u a f o

15. i t r e t f h o

IF YOU DON'T KNOW THE MEANING OF A WORD - LOOK IT UP. YOU NEED TO KNOW MEANINGS.

LEVEL 2 SPEELING QUIZ 4

1. fulfil
2. fulfilled
3. gauge
4. glamorous
5. government
6. harass
7. height
8. heir
9. honorary
10. humor
11. immediately
12. imminent
13. incidentally
14. install

T	G	L	A	M	O	R	O	U	S	W	O	B	W
F	E	G	O	V	E	R	N	M	E	N	T	J	A
I	N	C	I	D	E	N	T	A	L	L	Y	O	S
K	H	D	D	O	W	L	B	F	U	L	F	I	L
F	U	L	F	I	L	L	E	D	C	P	H	P	N
H	E	I	R	N	K	O	O	F	E	R	A	U	U
A	L	M	H	M	H	O	N	O	R	A	R	Y	Q
D	T	W	A	H	U	D	P	Z	Y	S	W	K	X
Q	U	Q	R	S	L	X	X	E	M	R	K	J	M
A	E	G	A	H	E	I	G	H	T	E	V	B	A
P	C	A	S	C	P	S	I	N	S	T	A	L	L
V	H	U	S	K	H	O	H	U	M	O	R	V	H
Y	I	G	I	M	M	E	D	I	A	T	E	L	Y
W	G	E	E	F	I	M	M	I	N	E	N	T	D

1. f u l f i l

2. l l i f d e l u f

3. g g e u a

4. a o o m s u r l g

5. n n o e t m g v r e

6. a a r h s s

7. g e i h h t

8. r i e h

9. o h y r o a r n

10. o h r m u

11. i d i e e t m l m y a

12. m i t n i e n m

13. n i a d c y l l i e t n

14. s l i t a l n

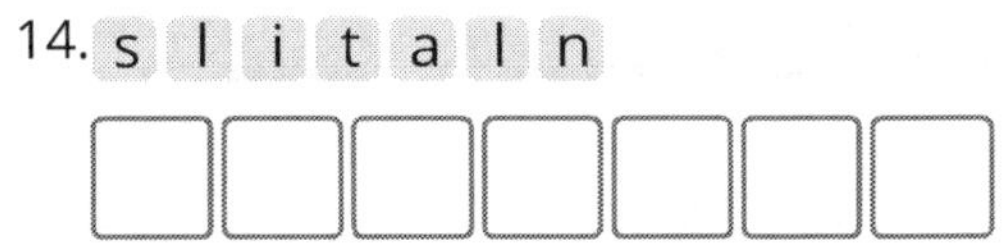

DO YOU KNOW HOW TO USE EACH OF THESE WORDS IN A SENTENCE? HAVE A GO!

LEVEL 2 SPELLING QUIZ 5

1. interested
2. irrelevant
3. knowledge
4. liaison
5. leisure
6. loose
7. maintain
8. maintenance
9. marvelous
10. miniature
11. miscellaneous
12. mischievous
13. necessarily
14. neighbor
15. ninth

U	X	B	H	Q	Z	R	M	O	Y	E	B	F	O	E	U
Y	M	S	E	T	K	N	O	W	L	E	D	G	E	F	H
S	A	H	M	I	N	I	A	T	U	R	E	Y	N	R	R
G	R	D	D	E	B	N	E	I	G	H	B	O	R	V	U
F	V	M	K	O	H	J	I	J	I	T	L	X	W	J	F
M	E	I	R	R	E	L	E	V	A	N	T	A	L	D	Y
A	L	E	V	D	N	E	C	E	S	S	A	R	I	L	Y
I	O	W	V	D	R	F	L	I	A	I	S	O	N	V	V
N	U	L	O	O	S	E	Y	E	S	E	N	R	M	Q	X
T	S	E	N	I	N	T	H	X	P	O	T	X	N	C	K
E	O	Q	S	L	E	I	S	U	R	E	Z	S	H	K	A
N	K	R	M	I	S	C	E	L	L	A	N	E	O	U	S
A	C	J	F	Q	I	Y	R	V	L	A	V	Y	P	A	M
N	C	M	I	S	C	H	I	E	V	O	U	S	R	E	B
C	M	G	I	N	T	E	R	E	S	T	E	D	J	I	F
E	E	K	D	M	A	I	N	T	A	I	N	W	L	B	H

1. t r e e s i t e d n

2. r l n e v i a e t r

3. e e n k w o l d g

4. s o a i l i n

5. u r i s l e e

6. o e o s l

7. i n t a m n i a

8. a e a t n n n m i c e

9. s l a m v r e o u

10. e t i m i n a u r

11. e o s a m s n u l e i c l

12. i i v h o e c m s u s

13. e s r s i a e n c l y

14. o g h b n r i e

15. n h i t n

NOW TRY TO WRITE A SENTENCE USING THREE OF THE NEW WORDS.

Level 2 Spelling Quiz 6

1. noticeable
2. nuisance
3. occasion
4. occur
5. occurrence
6. occurring
7. omission
8. opportunity
9. panicked
10. parallel
11. parliament
12. particularly
13. pastime
14. playwright
15. possess

F N G P O N O V X Y F G F C C P
Q U C L C M P L P M S M M F W A
W I O V C T P J A T P Q O Z J R
O S N N U T O L R N L E C D D T
C A H P R V R G L O A Z C P J I
C N P S R O T W I C Y N U Q Y C
U C A W I M U K A C W O R P T U
R E R U N I N N M A R T R O U L
P B A M G S I P E S I I E S G A
A U L O P S T A N I G C N S E R
S D L M Q I Y N T O H E C E Q L
T F E O P O R I F N T A E S G Y
I R L N N N M C B H U B W S R J
M S Z I P N R K Q R C L V Z C G
E A Y M X P D E C F Y E U Z N Z
R L A M X Y A D H V T E M E X P

Level 2 Spelling Quiz 6

TRY WRITING A PARAGRAPH USING AS MANY OF THE NEW WORDS AS YOU CAN.

1. n t l a i b o e e c

2. e s a c n i n u

3. n a s o o c i c

4. u r c o c

5. o c c e u n c r e r

6. u c c i r g r n o

7. n s s o o i i m

8. o y t u o t n p i p r

9. d i c e p n k a

10. l a l e p r l a

11. p r n m l e a a t i

12. t l c p y r a u l i a r

13. i t e a m p s

14. p a h i y g l r t w

15. e s s o s p s

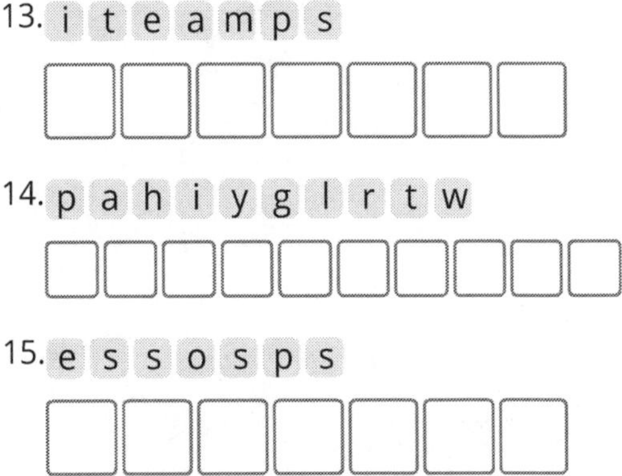

Level 2 Spelling Quiz 7

1. prefer
2. prejudice
3. premises
4. preparation
5. privilege
6. proceed
7. profession
8. prominent
9. publicly
10. pursue
11. quay
12. queue
13. quiet
14. quite
15. receipt

G	M	D	O	N	J	P	U	B	L	I	C	L	Y	A
V	L	P	L	K	Y	G	P	G	R	P	O	P	P	H
E	K	M	Z	L	D	S	G	Y	M	P	Q	W	R	P
Q	P	X	P	E	T	O	Z	T	P	R	U	F	O	E
P	M	U	R	O	U	F	R	Q	U	E	A	X	M	Q
R	T	D	E	X	X	E	R	E	R	J	Y	K	I	U
O	Q	U	P	R	M	Q	D	E	S	U	T	N	N	I
C	U	R	A	P	V	U	F	M	U	D	X	X	E	T
E	I	E	R	R	Z	E	U	I	E	I	U	W	N	E
E	C	C	A	E	E	U	G	C	Z	C	R	L	T	L
D	S	E	T	F	O	E	Q	B	W	E	J	X	B	G
P	U	I	I	E	S	O	P	R	E	M	I	S	E	S
Y	L	P	O	R	Q	U	I	E	T	V	A	E	N	I
G	C	T	N	Z	O	P	R	I	V	I	L	E	G	E
G	P	R	O	F	E	S	S	I	O	N	B	Q	O	P

Level 2 Spelling Quiz 7

GO THROUGH THE LIST OF WORDS AND CROSS OUT THE WORDS YOU KNOW. LEARN THE OTHERS.

1. e p r f r e

2. i d r u j e p c e

3. s i e e r s m p

4. n i r p p e a t r a o

5. e l r i v e p g i

6. c d e r e p o

7. p o s f r e n s o i

8. e n r i m t p n o

9. y i b l u c l p

10. u p u s e r

11. y a q u

12. u q e e u

13. e q i t u

14. t q i e u

15. e t p e i r c

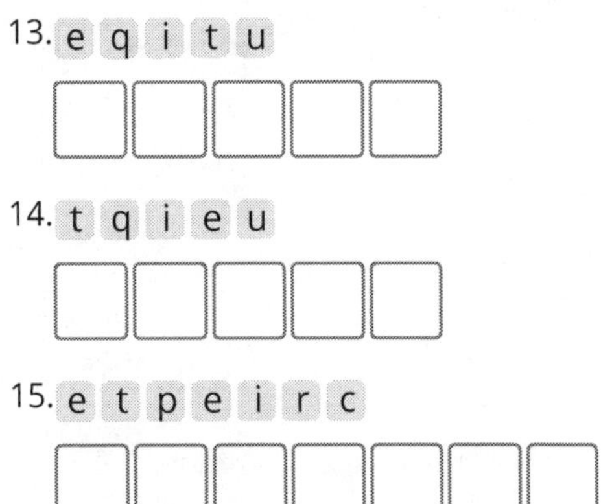

Level 2 Spelling Quiz 8

1. receive
2. recommend
3. relevant
4. schedule
5. scissors
6. seize
7. separate
8. siege
9. skilful
10. stationery
11. stationary
12. strength
13. succeed
14. surprise
15. temporary

X S V J B S K I L F U L V P R
V T J S P S T C S I S Z J W L
O A M T R T E S F I C H N S Q
K T V R E A M U H K I M T U H
K I F E C T P C O U S Y R R J
J O P N E I O C J C S C E P R
C N Y G I O R E S F O S C R E
B A H T V N A E E S R I O I L
N R N H E E R D P C S E M S E
S Y R N E R Y V A H H G M E V
E K Y P O Y I G R E M E E D A
I W P Z Q E Y Q A D N N N X N
Z T N O R P K P T U B M D R T
E F H W K Y S R E L S C Y R E
P B S L K M J T Q E T E M Q K

Level 2 Spelling Quiz 8

USE A DICTIONARY TO LOOK UP THE WORDS YOU DO NOT KNOW ALPHABETICALLY.

1. r e e e c i v

2. n m r e o d m e c

3. t e l e r v n a

4. e c h e s d l u

5. s c i s s s r o

6. z e e i s

7. e e p a s r t a

8. g i e e s

9. s l k l i f u

10. n e y t a r o t s i

11. n a y t a r o t s i

12. h t r e s n t g

13. s d u c c e e

14. e u r p s r s i

15. r r t a p y o e m

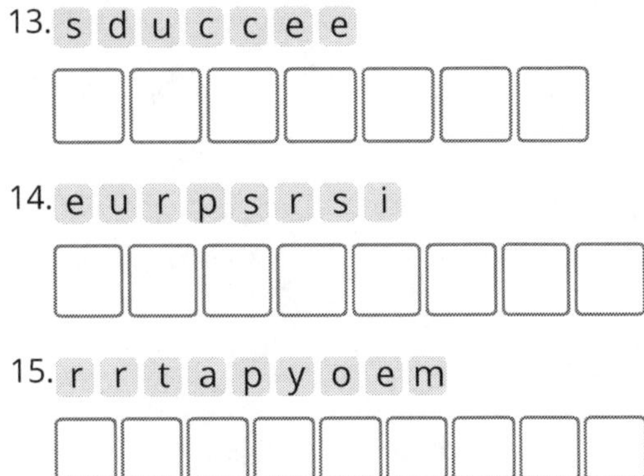

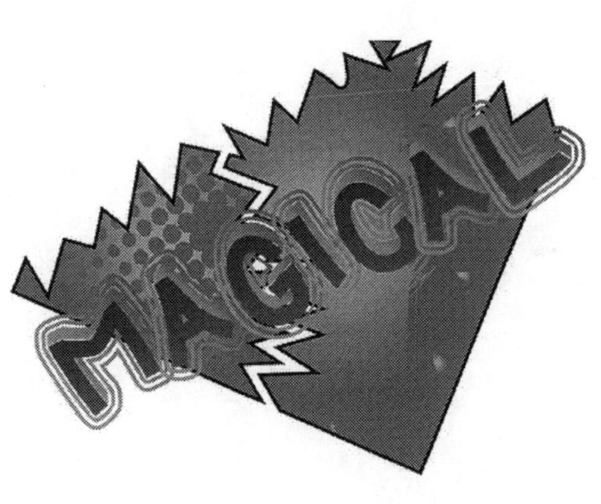

Level 2 Spelling Quiz 9

1. temporary	2. tendency	3. tragedy	4. twelfth
5. unnecessary	6. unparalleled	7. until	8. vicious
9. vigorous	10. vinegar	11. waist	12. waste
13. wednesday	14. weird	15. wired	

G	W	A	I	S	T	R	Z	E	A	V	S	M	G	U
U	N	P	A	R	A	L	L	E	L	E	D	S	H	U
D	Y	D	J	T	C	M	T	Y	H	Y	P	A	X	E
O	K	T	X	E	U	A	G	L	T	G	Q	Z	N	J
W	K	N	W	M	N	O	T	V	I	C	I	O	U	S
I	F	T	K	P	N	Z	D	F	X	K	Y	K	D	X
R	P	R	T	O	E	B	P	P	W	A	S	T	E	D
E	V	A	W	R	C	T	M	H	G	W	E	I	R	D
D	I	G	E	A	E	V	I	G	O	R	O	U	S	J
U	N	E	L	R	S	W	E	D	N	E	S	D	A	Y
N	E	D	F	Y	S	Q	O	O	S	W	R	V	M	H
T	G	Y	T	K	A	T	E	N	D	E	N	C	Y	O
I	A	H	H	D	R	X	E	D	G	Y	Y	D	T	X
L	R	S	E	G	Y	P	I	R	T	Q	Y	I	T	P
A	L	H	P	C	I	K	M	A	Z	M	X	F	T	L

Level 2 Spelling Quiz 9

TRY COMING UP WITH A SYNONYM FOR EACH OF THESE NEW WORDS. GOOD LUCK!

1. r m o e r a t y p

2. n y e e t d c n

3. e t a y r d g

4. f t e h w t l

5. s r y n s e n a c u e

6. a r e d u p e l l l n a

7. i l u t n

8. o v c s i u i

9. g s i r v o u o

10. g v n r i a e

11. s t w i a

12. t e w s a

13. a d e e s d w y n

14. r d w i e

15. e d w r i

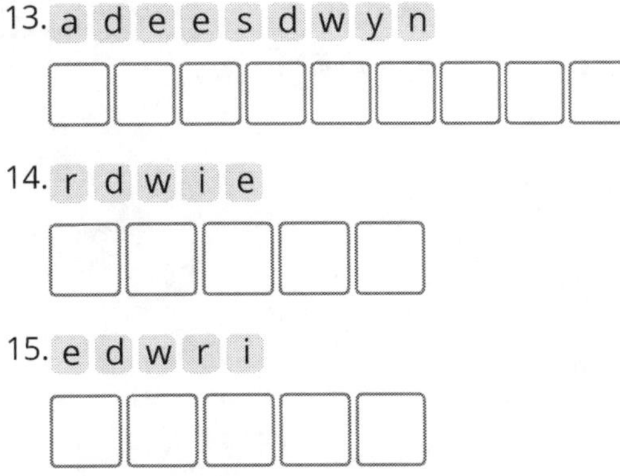

Level 2 punctuation

1. what do you use before but and because

A [ ] apostrophe B [ ] full stop
C [X] comma D [ ] question mark

2. when do you use a apostrophe

A [ ] ending a sentence
B [ ] replacing a conjunction
C [ ] sentence starters
D [X] replacing a letter don't can't

3. what do you use a semicolon for

A [X] replacing a conjunction
B [ ] starting a list
C [ ] starting or ending speech
D [ ] separating a sentence

4. what do you put when you start a list

A [ ] apostrophe B [X] colon
C [ ] semicolon D [ ] comma

5. what do you use a question mark for

A [ ] being angry at someone
B [X] asking a question
C [ ] replacing a conjunction
D [ ] starting a list

6. when do you a exclamation mark

A [ ] separating a sentence
B [ ] ending a sentence
C [X] when are yelling at someone
D [ ] replacing a conjunction

7. what do you put at the end of a sentence

A [ ] comma B [ ] semicolon
C [ ] question mark D [X] full stop

8. what do you sometimes use at a end of a paragraph

A [X] ellipsis B [ ] exclamation mark
C [ ] apostrophe D [ ] colon

Level 2 Punctuation 2

“ ”		Full stop
•••		Comma
?		Apostrophe
'		Capital letters
!		Speech marks
,		Question mark
ABC		Exclamation mark
●		Ellipses

Level 2 Punctuation 3

1. creates a pause or breaks up ideas

A [ ] ! exclamation marks
B [ ] - dash
C [ ] ? question mark
D [X] , commas

2. shows expression or importance

A [ ] - dash
B [ ] ; semi colon
C [X] ! exclamation marks
D [ ] ... ellipsis

3. adds extra information which isn't necessarily needed

A [ ] ; semi colon B [X] ( ) brackets
C [ ] ? question mark D [ ] ... ellipsis

4. signals a cliffhanger or shows words are missing

A [X] ... ellipsis B [ ] : colon
C [ ] ( ) brackets D [ ] ' apostrophe

5. shows a question

A [X] ? question mark
B [ ] ( ) brackets
C [ ] ' ' inverted comma
D [ ] ... ellipsis

6. used before a phrase which sums up a sentence or either side of a dropped in idea

A [ ] ; semi colon B [ ] , commas
C [X] - dash D [ ] ! exclamation marks

7. introduces a list or links sentences that explain each other

A [X] : colon B [ ] - dash
C [ ] ( ) brackets D [ ] ! exclamation marks

8. links two sentences often replacing and or but, seperates items in a long list

A [ ] ! exclamation marks B [X] ; semi colon
C [ ] ( ) brackets D [ ] , commas

9. shows a word is informal or shows evidence from a text

A [ ] ' apostrophe
B [X] ' ' inverted comma
C [ ] ! exclamation marks
D [ ] ( ) brackets

10. shows possession or a contraction

A [ ] - dash
B [X] ' apostrophe
C [ ] ' ' inverted comma
D [ ] ... ellipsis

Level 2 Punctuation 4

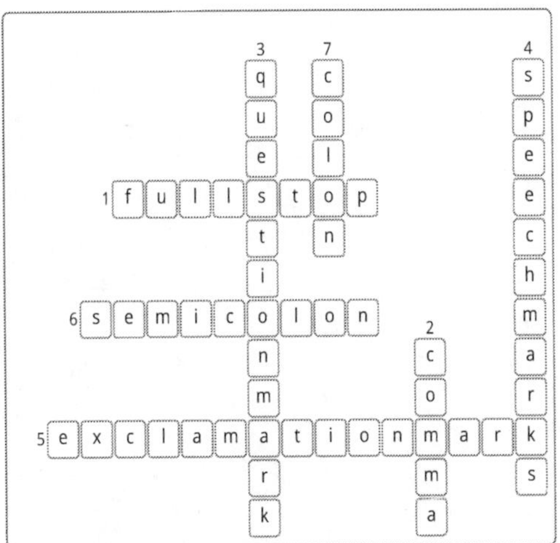

Across

1. This shows that a sentence has ended (4,4)
5. used to show anger or excitement (11,4)
6. to replace a connective and separate two linked clauses (9)

Down

2. Used to separate clauses within a sentence (5)
3. At the end of an interrogative (8,4)
4. used for speech or quotations (6,5)
7. to introduce a list (5)

Level 2 Punctuation 5

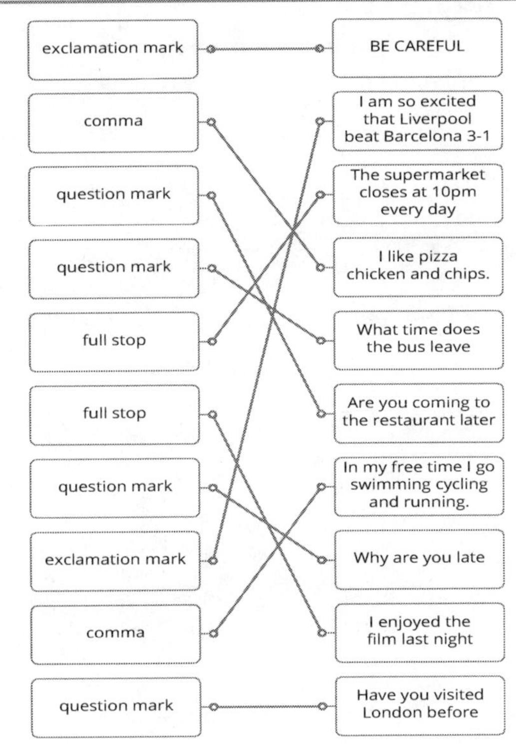

Level 2 Types of Text

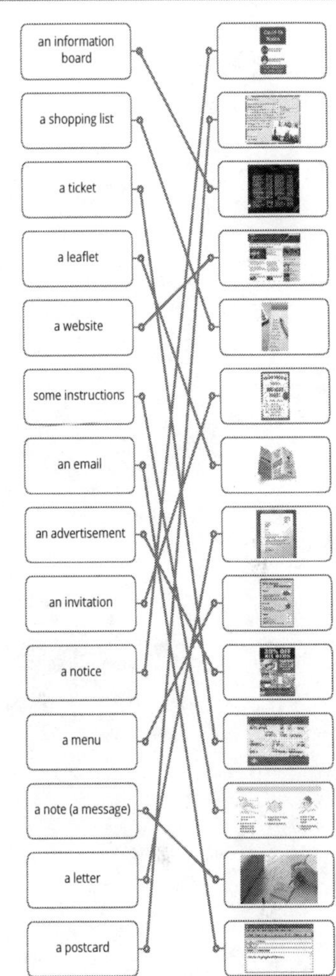

LEVEL 2 SKIMMING AND SCANNING

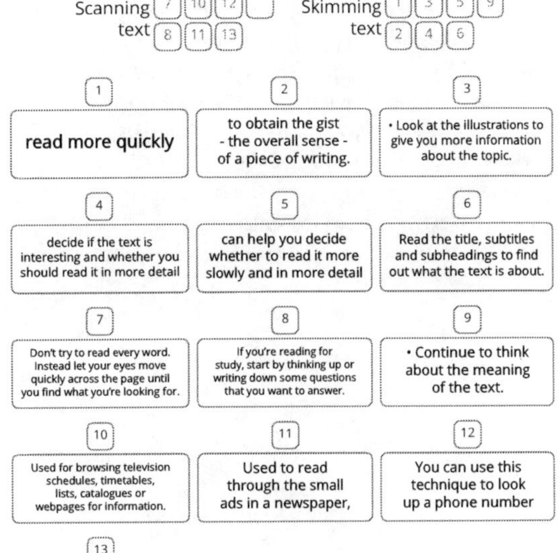

Level 2 Conjunctions quiz

1. I didn't do my homework__________ my dog ate it!

A [X] because B [ ] so C [ ] and

2. It was sunny outside__________ we went out to play.

A [ ] but B [X] so C [ ] because

3. I was late __________ my car didn't start.

A [ ] and B [ ] but C [X] because

4. I went to the shop__________ bought some fruit.

A [X] and B [ ] if C [ ] so

5. I opened the door __________ someone was knocking.

A [ ] but B [ ] and C [X] because

6. Ben fell over __________ he was not hurt.

A [X] but B [ ] because C [ ] if

7. The dog barked __________ wagged his tail

A [ ] because B [ ] so C [X] and

8. I like apples __________ I don't like oranges.

A [X] but B [ ] because C [ ] and

9. You should install street lights _____ it is safer.

A [X] so B [ ] but C [ ] and

10. You should install CCTV __________ it will cost quite a lot of money.

A [ ] because B [X] although C [ ] so

11. You will get wet, ___ you go out in the rain

A [X] if B [ ] but C [ ] so

12. I had a great day, __________ I felt tired in the evening.

A [ ] so B [ ] because C [X] although

13. We hoped to have a nice day: __________ the children were really naughty

A [ ] so B [X] however C [ ] and

14. I went to the reception _____ I arrived.

A [X] when B [ ] because C [ ] so

15. I mopped the floor __________ I stopped to have my lunch

A [ ] but B [ ] because C [X] before

NOW

Active v Passive Sentences

Larry generously donated money to the homeless shelter.
Nobody responded to my sales ad.
The Wedding Planner will make all the reservations.
Susan will bake two dozen cookies for the sale.
The science class viewed the comet.
The cleaning crew vacuum and dust the office every night.
The teacher always answers the students questions.
The workers paved the entire stretch of road.
I ran the obstacle course in record time.

Level 2 Conjunctions Whack a Mole

But ✓ | So ✓ | However ✓ | My
I | Time | Biggest | Smaller
Express | And ✓ | Happy | Cheerfully
After ✓ | In | For ✓

Level 2 Sentence types

1. Curiosity killed the cat.

A [X] Simple sentence B [ ] Complex sentence C [ ] Compound sentence

2. The car swerved to miss Mrs Jackson, who had slipped off the pavement.

A [ ] Simple sentence B [X] Complex sentence C [ ] Compound sentence

3. I like tea, and he likes coffee.

A [ ] Simple sentence B [ ] Complex sentence C [X] Compound sentence

4. I always wanted to be somebody, but I should have been more specific.

A [ ] Simple sentence B [ ] Complex sentence C [X] Compound sentence

5. She ran quickly but still did not catch the escaping puppy

A [ ] Simple sentence B [ ] Complex sentence C [X] Compound sentence

6. She returned the computer after she noticed it was damaged.

A [ ] Simple sentence B [X] Complex sentence C [ ] Compound sentence

7. The movie, though very long, was still very enjoyable.

A [ ] Simple sentence B [X] Complex sentence C [ ] Compound sentence

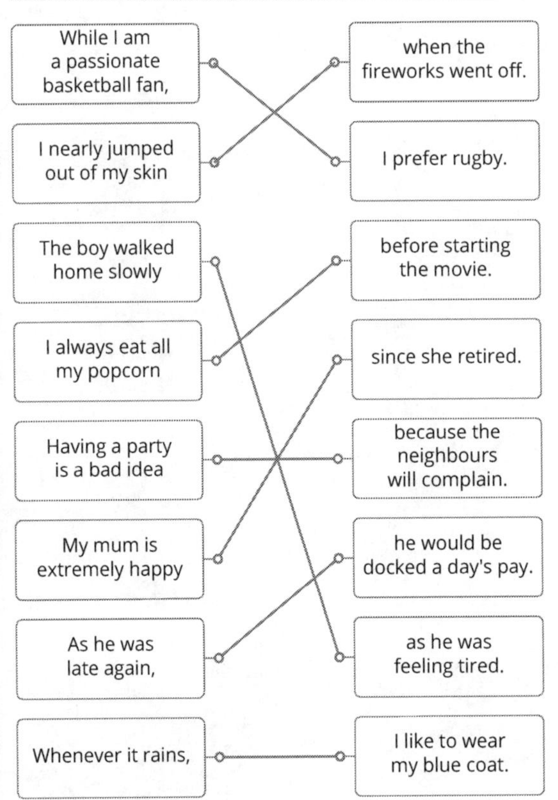

Grammar Quiz 1

Correct: My friend and I are going to the movies.

Correct: The book's cover is red.

Correct: I don't have any time to do my homework.

Correct: They were playing soccer in the park.

Correct: I saw that movie last night.

Correct: She doesn't want any of those cookies.

Correct: The cat lay on the couch all day.

Correct: I can hardly wait for the party.

Correct: The students don't seem interested in the topic.

Correct: He doesn't know how to swim.

Grammar Quiz 2

Corrected:
John is a college student. He studies at a prestigious university in the city. Yesterday, John went to the library to study for his upcoming exams. He sat at a table and took out his textbook. John opened the book and began to read. After a few minutes, his friends came into the library. They sat next to him and started talking loudly. John got annoyed because he couldn't concentrate. He asked them to be quiet, but they ignored him.

Corrected:
John decided to go for a walk to clear his mind. He walked through the campus and saw a group of students playing frisbee. He watched them for a while and thought about joining, but he didn't have a frisbee. John saw a friend across the field and waved at them. They waved back and called him over. John walked towards them and they gave him a frisbee to join the game. They all had a lot of fun playing together.

Corrected:
Later that evening, John went to a coffee shop to meet his study group. They discussed their project and assigned tasks to each other. John volunteered to write the introduction while the others worked on the research. They stayed at the coffee shop for several hours, working hard on their assignments. Finally, they finished their work and felt satisfied with their progress. They planned to meet again next week to finalise the project.

Level 2 Capital letters

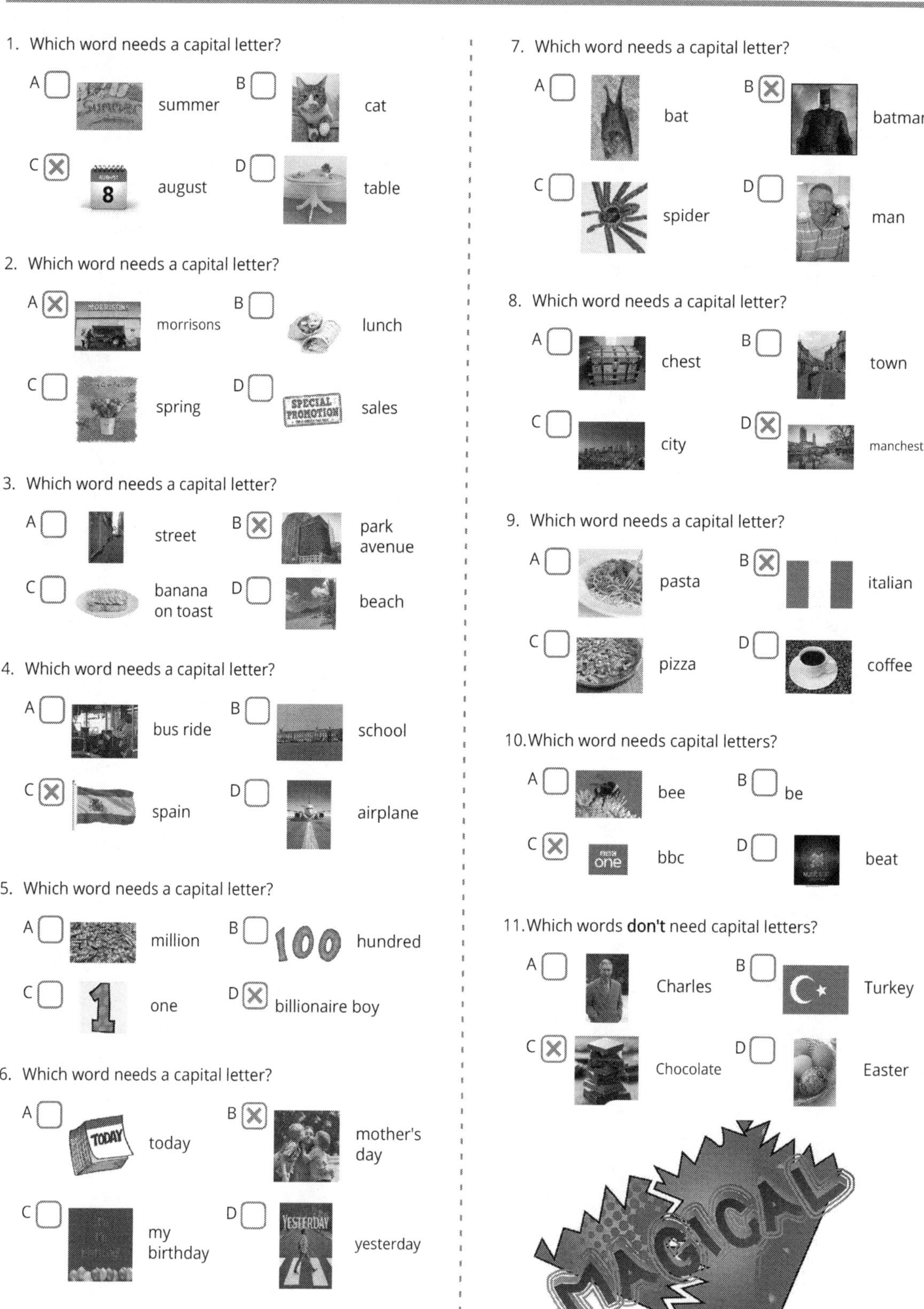

1. Which word needs a capital letter?
   - A [ ] summer
   - B [ ] cat
   - C [x] august
   - D [ ] table

2. Which word needs a capital letter?
   - A [x] morrisons
   - B [ ] lunch
   - C [ ] spring
   - D [ ] sales

3. Which word needs a capital letter?
   - A [ ] street
   - B [x] park avenue
   - C [ ] banana on toast
   - D [ ] beach

4. Which word needs a capital letter?
   - A [ ] bus ride
   - B [ ] school
   - C [x] spain
   - D [ ] airplane

5. Which word needs a capital letter?
   - A [ ] million
   - B [ ] hundred
   - C [ ] one
   - D [x] billionaire boy

6. Which word needs a capital letter?
   - A [ ] today
   - B [x] mother's day
   - C [ ] my birthday
   - D [ ] yesterday

7. Which word needs a capital letter?
   - A [ ] bat
   - B [x] batman
   - C [ ] spider
   - D [ ] man

8. Which word needs a capital letter?
   - A [ ] chest
   - B [ ] town
   - C [ ] city
   - D [x] manchester

9. Which word needs a capital letter?
   - A [ ] pasta
   - B [x] italian
   - C [ ] pizza
   - D [ ] coffee

10. Which word needs capital letters?
    - A [ ] bee
    - B [ ] be
    - C [x] bbc
    - D [ ] beat

11. Which words **don't** need capital letters?
    - A [ ] Charles
    - B [ ] Turkey
    - C [x] Chocolate
    - D [ ] Easter

Level 2 Grammar Quiz 3

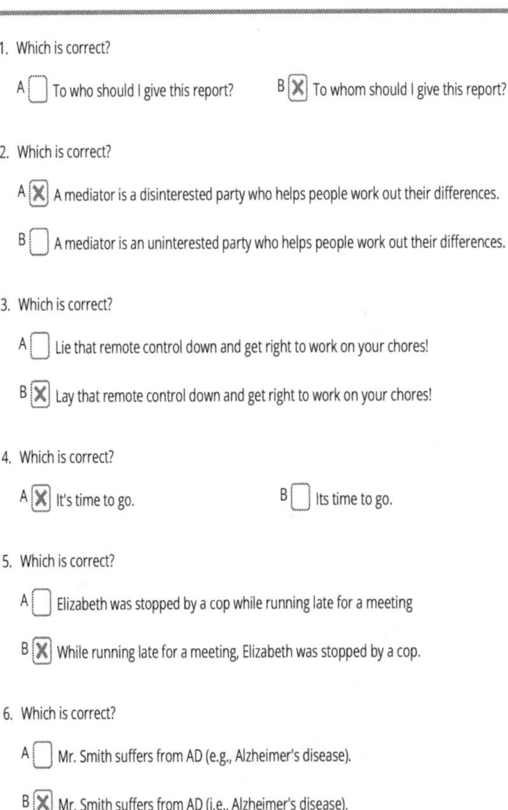

1. Which is correct?

   A ☐ To who should I give this report? B ☒ To whom should I give this report?

2. Which is correct?

   A ☒ A mediator is a disinterested party who helps people work out their differences.

   B ☐ A mediator is an uninterested party who helps people work out their differences.

3. Which is correct?

   A ☐ Lie that remote control down and get right to work on your chores!

   B ☒ Lay that remote control down and get right to work on your chores!

4. Which is correct?

   A ☒ It's time to go. B ☐ Its time to go.

5. Which is correct?

   A ☐ Elizabeth was stopped by a cop while running late for a meeting

   B ☒ While running late for a meeting, Elizabeth was stopped by a cop.

6. Which is correct?

   A ☐ Mr. Smith suffers from AD (e.g., Alzheimer's disease).

   B ☒ Mr. Smith suffers from AD (i.e., Alzheimer's disease).

7. Which is correct?

   A ☐ We'll get much farther if we can talk about this rationally.

   B ☒ We'll get much further if we can talk about this rationally.

Level 2 Homophones Quiz

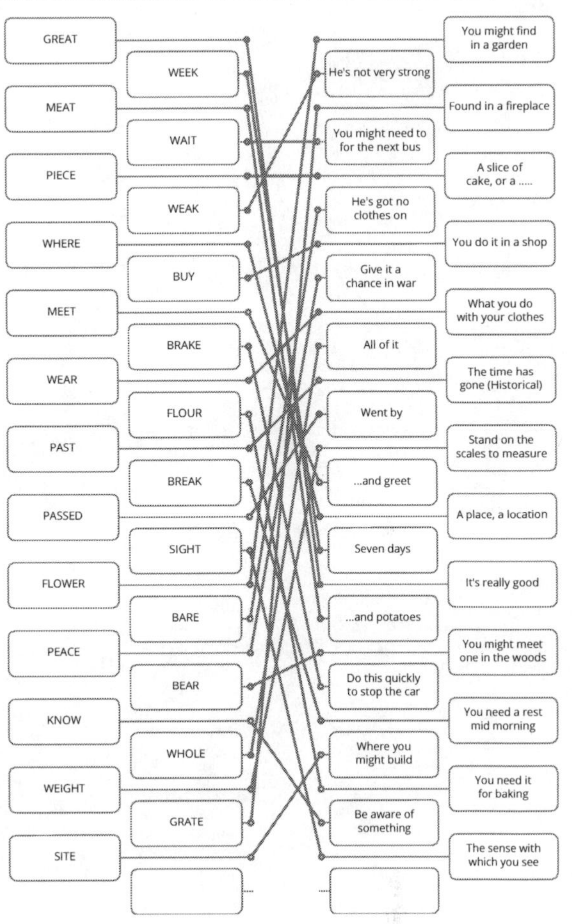

Level 2 Homophones Crossword

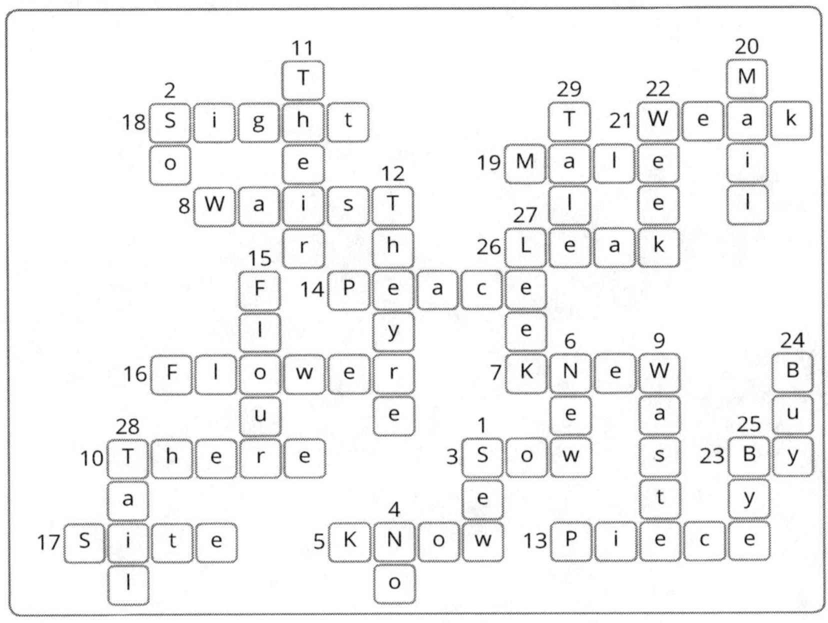

Level 2 Synonyms Quiz

nervous	courageous
hungry	breakable
dark	ravenous
fragile	gloomy
thirsty	dazzling
rich	feeble
brave	anxious
strong	parched
bright	powerful
weak	wealthy

Level 2 Dictionary Corner - Use a dictionary to find a word with a similar meaning

1. The **diligent** student received an A on the exam.
   A [X] hardworking B [ ] apathetic C [ ] lazy

2. The detective **carefully** examined the crime scene.
   A [ ] haphazardly B [ ] carelessly C [X] meticulously

3. The chef prepared a **delicious** meal for the guests.
   A [ ] tasteless B [X] tasty C [ ] repulsive

4. The athlete demonstrated exceptional **agility** during the game.
   A [X] nimbleness B [ ] clumsiness C [ ] sluggishness

5. The teacher used **innovative** methods to engage the students.
   A [ ] conventional B [ ] outdated C [X] creative

6. The speaker delivered a **persuasive** argument to the audience.
   A [ ] nonsensical B [X] compelling C [ ] incoherent

7. The artist exhibited her **stunning** artwork at the gallery.
   A [ ] unimpressive B [ ] mediocre C [X] impressive

8. The scientist conducted **extensive** research for the project.
   A [X] thorough B [ ] superficial C [ ] incomplete

9. The team **collaborated** effectively to complete the task.
   A [ ] competed B [X] cooperated C [ ] conflicted

10. The author crafted a **captivating** story that kept readers hooked.
   A [ ] uninteresting B [ ] tedious C [X] engrossing

Level 2 Inference vocabulary

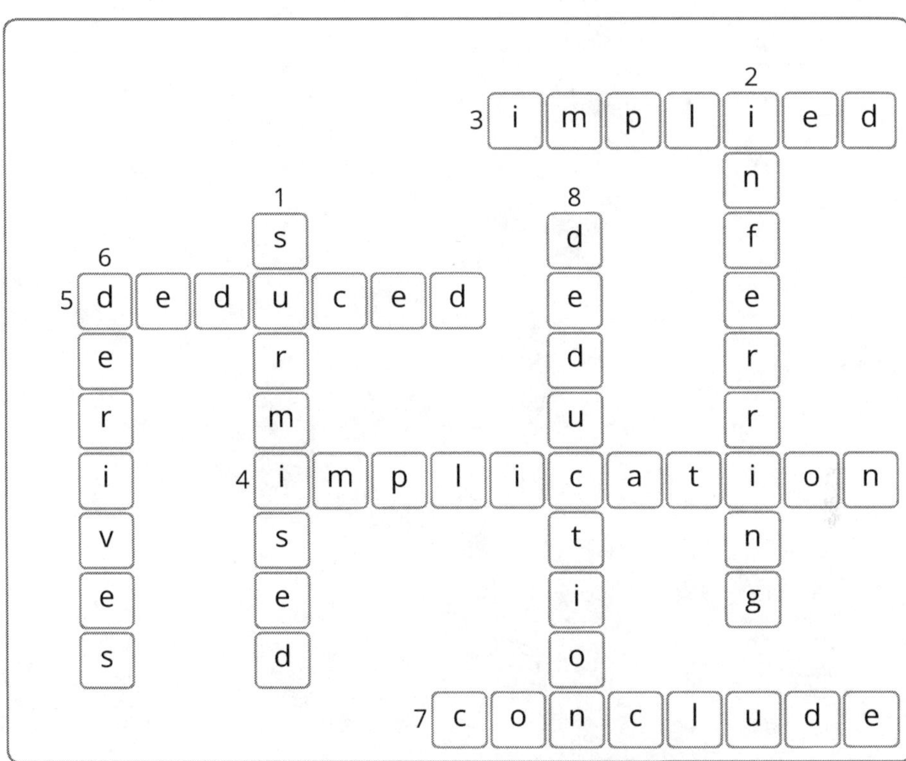

Level 2 Inference Quiz 1

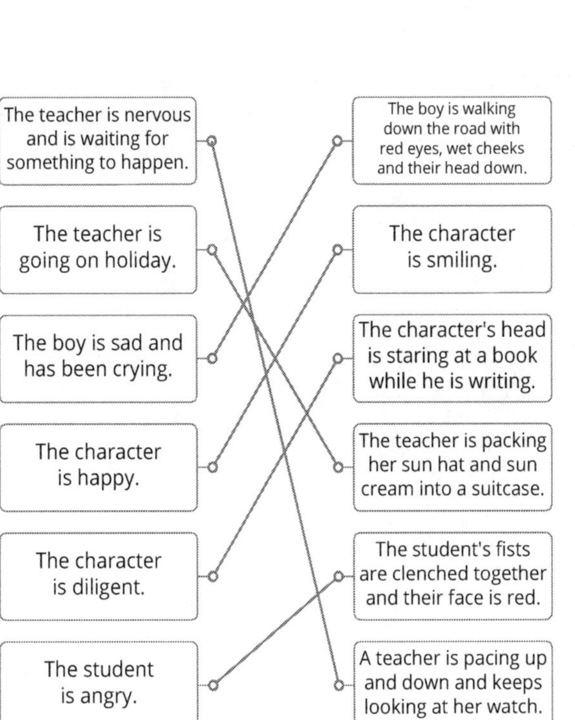

Level 2 Organisational Features

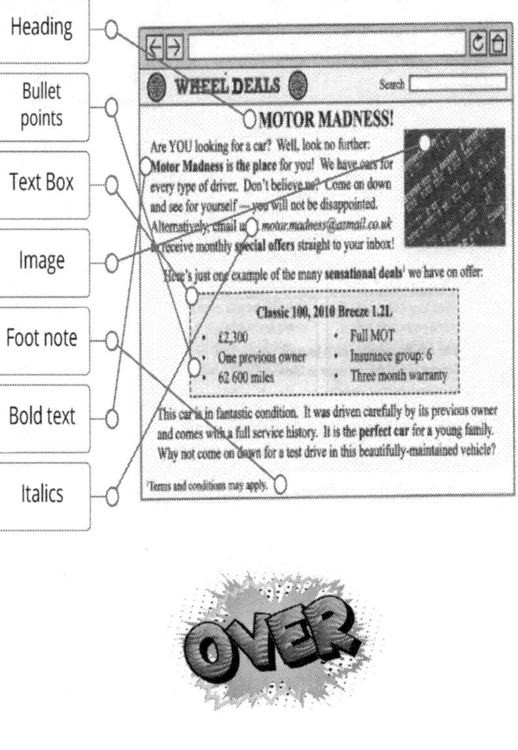

Level 2 Organisational Features Quiz 1

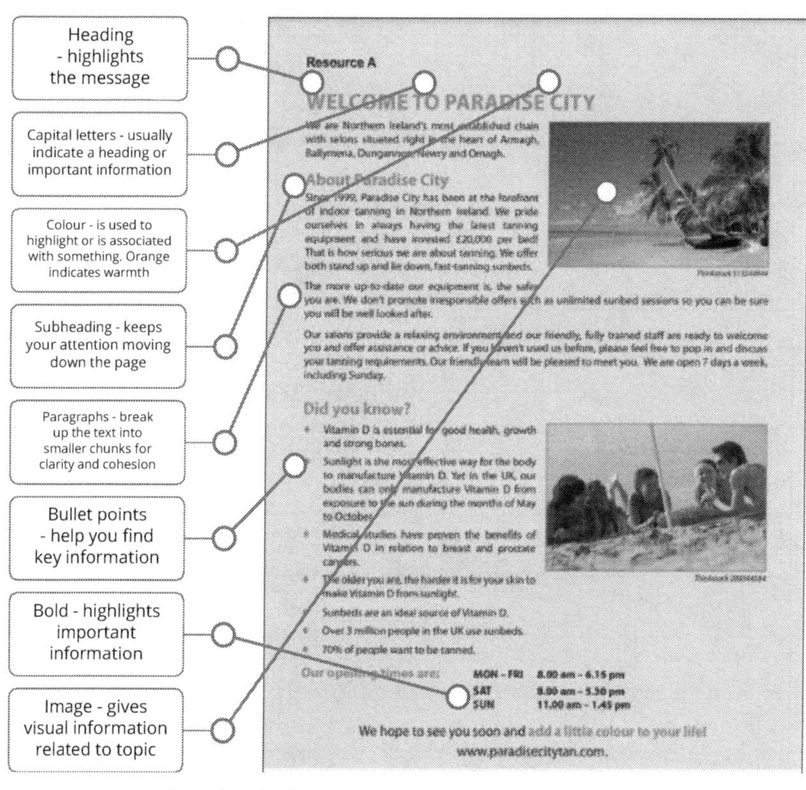

Resource A

WELCOME TO PARADISE CITY

We are Northern Ireland's most established chain with salons situated right in the heart of Armagh, Ballymena, Dungannon, Newry and Omagh.

About Paradise City

Since 1999, Paradise City has been at the forefront of indoor tanning in Northern Ireland. We pride ourselves in always having the latest tanning equipment and have invested £20,000 per bed! That is how serious we are about tanning. We offer both stand up and lie down, fast-tanning sunbeds.

The more up-to-date our equipment is, the safer you are. We don't promote irresponsible offers such as unlimited sunbed sessions so you can be sure you will be well looked after.

Our salons provide a relaxing environment and our friendly, fully trained staff are ready to welcome you and offer assistance or advice. If you haven't used us before, please feel free to pop in and discuss your tanning requirements. Our friendly team will be pleased to meet you. We are open 7 days a week, including Sunday.

Did you know?

- Vitamin D is essential for good health, growth and strong bones.
- Sunlight is the most effective way for the body to manufacture Vitamin D. Yet in the UK, our bodies can only manufacture Vitamin D from exposure to the sun during the months of May to October.
- Medical studies have proven the benefits of Vitamin D in relation to breast and prostate cancers.
- The older you are, the harder it is for your skin to make Vitamin D from sunlight.
- Sunbeds are an ideal source of Vitamin D.
- Over 3 million people in the UK use sunbeds.
- 70% of people want to be tanned.

Our opening times are:

MON - FRI	**8.00 am - 6.15 pm**
SAT	**8.00 am - 5.30 pm**
SUN	**11.00 am - 1.45 pm**

We hope to see you soon and add a little colour to your life!

www.paradisecitytan.com.

Letter Level 2 Quiz 1

Draw a line from each of the elements of the letter to the position they should go.

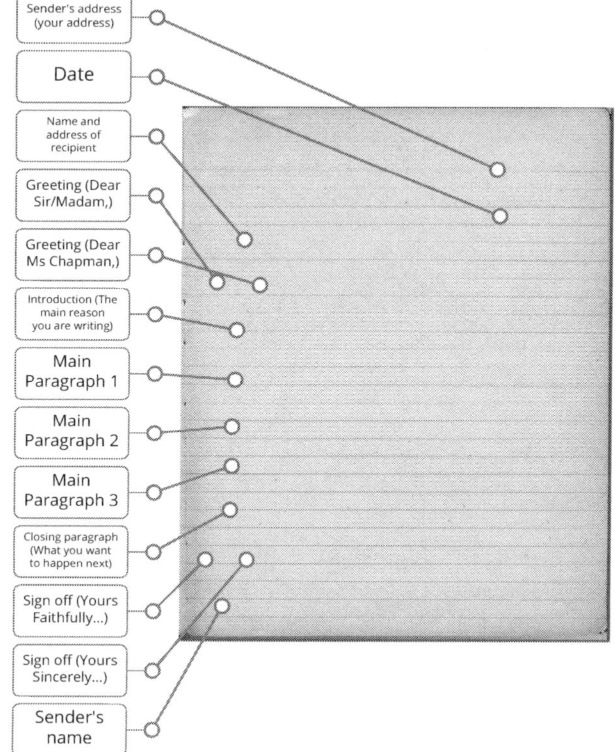

Organisational Features

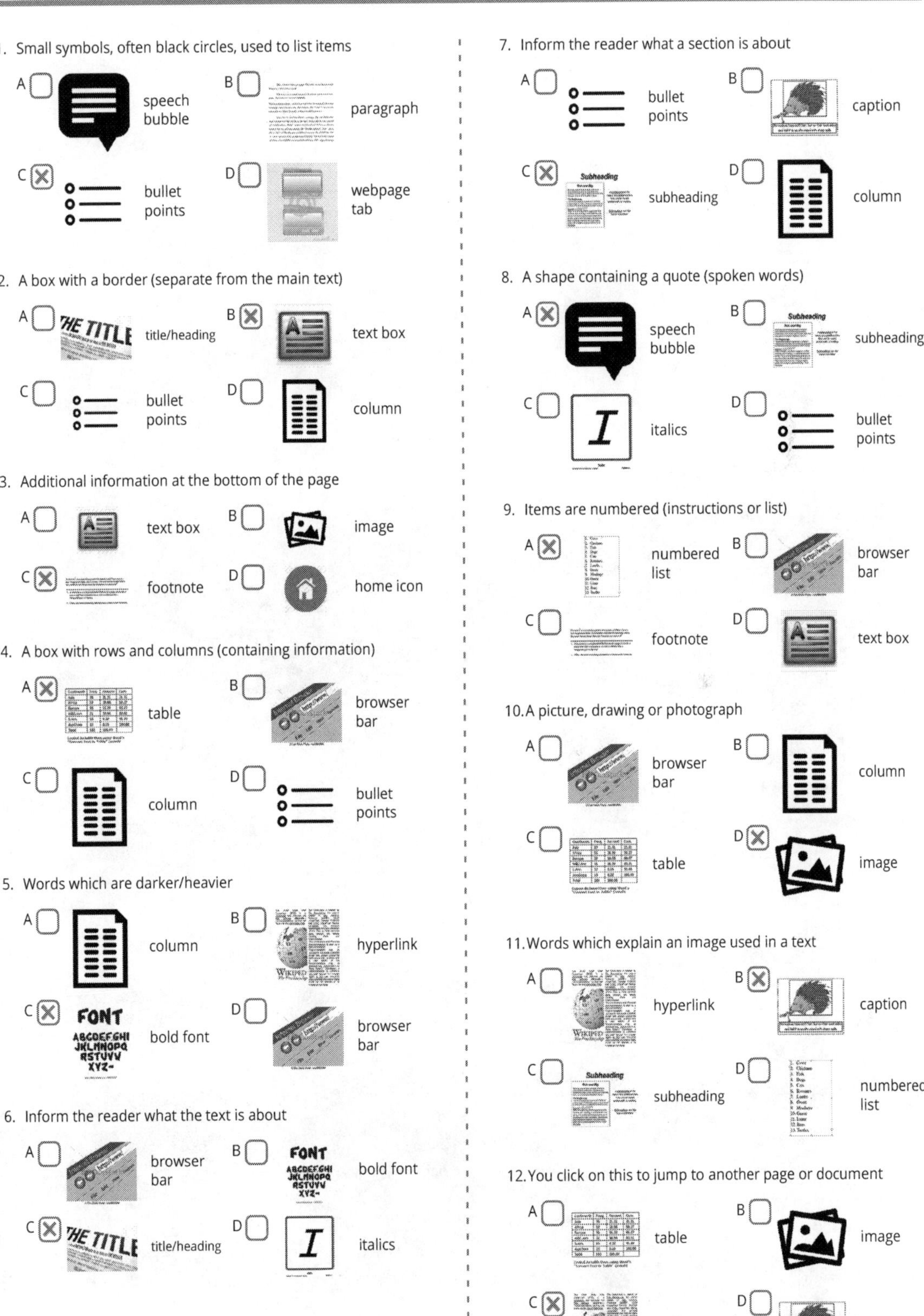

1. Small symbols, often black circles, used to list items
   - [ ] A speech bubble
   - [ ] B paragraph
   - [x] C bullet points
   - [ ] D webpage tab

2. A box with a border (separate from the main text)
   - [ ] A title/heading
   - [x] B text box
   - [ ] C bullet points
   - [ ] D column

3. Additional information at the bottom of the page
   - [ ] A text box
   - [ ] B image
   - [x] C footnote
   - [ ] D home icon

4. A box with rows and columns (containing information)
   - [x] A table
   - [ ] B browser bar
   - [ ] C column
   - [ ] D bullet points

5. Words which are darker/heavier
   - [ ] A column
   - [ ] B hyperlink
   - [x] C bold font
   - [ ] D browser bar

6. Inform the reader what the text is about
   - [ ] A browser bar
   - [ ] B bold font
   - [x] C title/heading
   - [ ] D italics

7. Inform the reader what a section is about
   - [ ] A bullet points
   - [ ] B caption
   - [x] C subheading
   - [ ] D column

8. A shape containing a quote (spoken words)
   - [x] A speech bubble
   - [ ] B subheading
   - [ ] C italics
   - [ ] D bullet points

9. Items are numbered (instructions or list)
   - [x] A numbered list
   - [ ] B browser bar
   - [ ] C footnote
   - [ ] D text box

10. A picture, drawing or photograph
    - [ ] A browser bar
    - [ ] B column
    - [ ] C table
    - [x] D image

11. Words which explain an image used in a text
    - [ ] A hyperlink
    - [x] B caption
    - [ ] C subheading
    - [ ] D numbered list

12. You click on this to jump to another page or document
    - [ ] A table
    - [ ] B image
    - [x] C hyperlink
    - [ ] D caption

Level 2 Letter Writing Quiz

1. A letter written to a friend is known as
   - A ☐ a formal letter
   - B ☐ a business letter
   - C ☒ an informal letter
   - D ☐ a letter of application

2. The first item on the top right of a letter is
   - A ☐ the recipient's address
   - B ☐ reference to what you are writing about
   - C ☐ the greeting or salutation
   - D ☒ sender's address

3. You should greet your friend as
   - A ☐ Dear Sir
   - B ☐ Dear..........(surname)
   - C ☒ Dear ....(first name)
   - D ☐ Dear Madam

4. The information that follows in your letter should be written
   - A ☒ in paragraphs
   - B ☐ in columns
   - C ☐ a chapter
   - D ☐ one block

5. You begin a new paragraph when
   - A ☐ you start a new sentence
   - B ☒ you change to a new idea
   - C ☐ you have more of the same information
   - D ☐ you explain a point

6. You close an informal letter with
   - A ☐ yours sincerely
   - B ☐ yours faithfully
   - C ☒ love/best wishes
   - D ☐ yours in hope

Level 2 Formal Email Layout

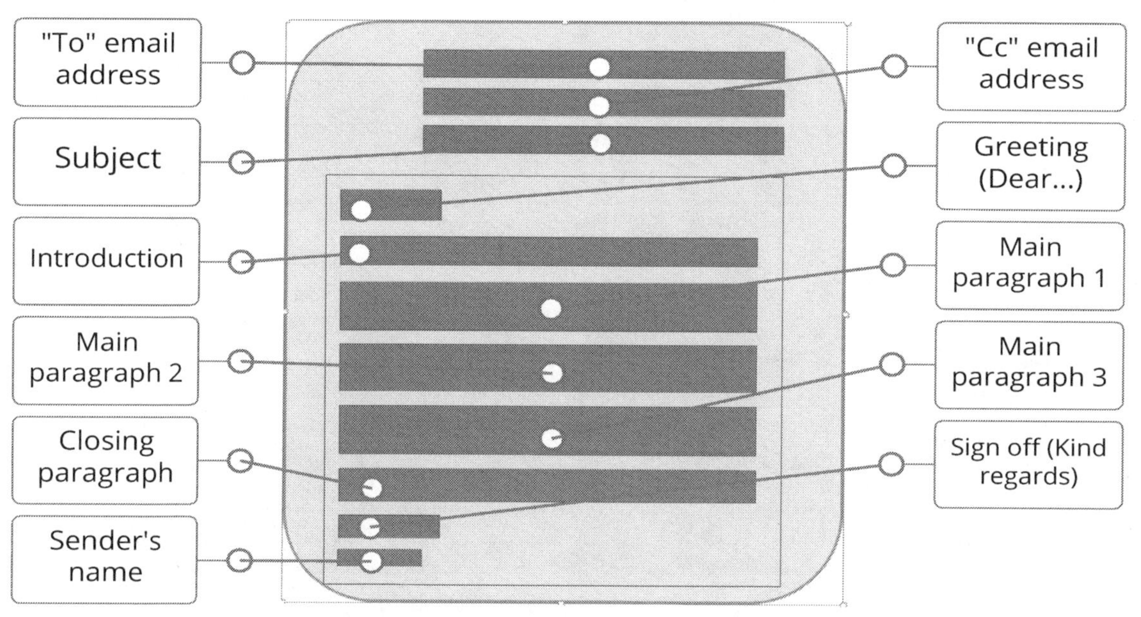

Level 2 Review- layout

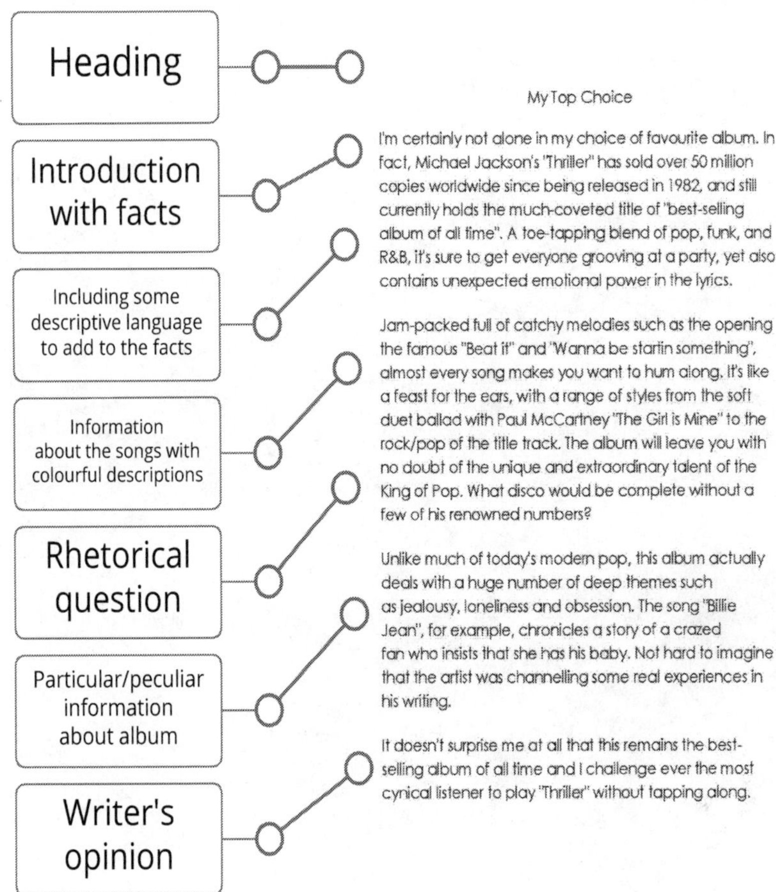

My Top Choice

I'm certainly not alone in my choice of favourite album. In fact, Michael Jackson's "Thriller" has sold over 50 million copies worldwide since being released in 1982, and still currently holds the much-coveted title of "best-selling album of all time". A toe-tapping blend of pop, funk, and R&B, it's sure to get everyone grooving at a party, yet also contains unexpected emotional power in the lyrics.

Jam-packed full of catchy melodies such as the opening the famous "Beat it" and "Wanna be startin something", almost every song makes you want to hum along. It's like a feast for the ears, with a range of styles from the soft duet ballad with Paul McCartney "The Girl is Mine" to the rock/pop of the title track. The album will leave you with no doubt of the unique and extraordinary talent of the King of Pop. What disco would be complete without a few of his renowned numbers?

Unlike much of today's modern pop, this album actually deals with a huge number of deep themes such as jealousy, loneliness and obsession. The song "Billie Jean", for example, chronicles a story of a crazed fan who insists that she has his baby. Not hard to imagine that the artist was channelling some real experiences in his writing.

It doesn't surprise me at all that this remains the best-selling album of all time and I challenge ever the most cynical listener to play "Thriller" without tapping along.

Level 2 Writing an Application

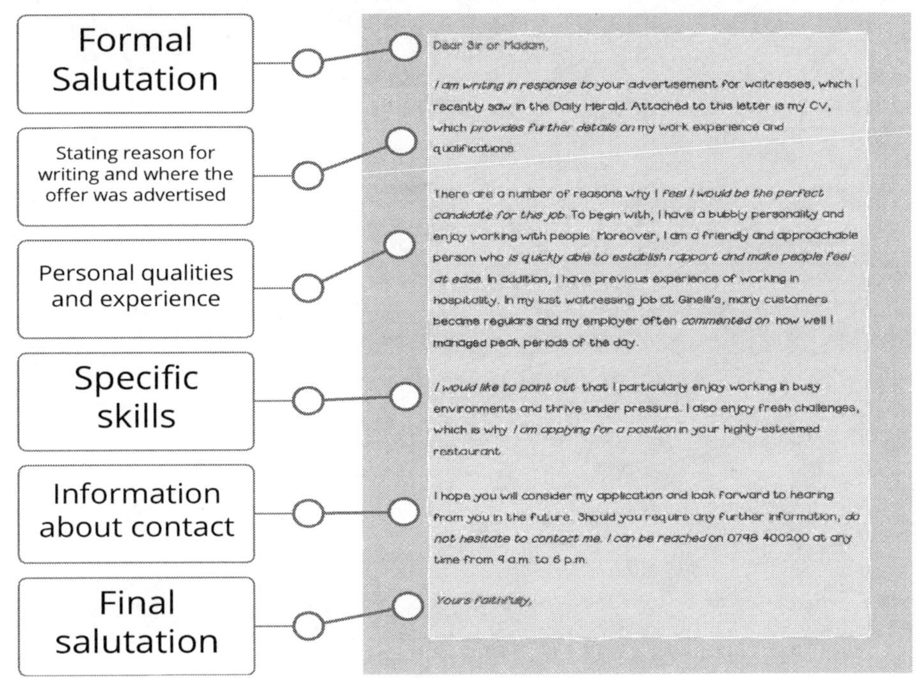

Dear Sir or Madam,

I am writing in response to your advertisement for waitresses, which I recently saw in the Daily Herald. Attached to this letter is my CV, which *provides further details on* my work experience and qualifications.

There are a number of reasons why I *feel I would be the perfect candidate for this job*. To begin with, I have a bubbly personality and enjoy working with people. Moreover, I am a friendly and approachable person who *is quickly able to establish rapport and make people feel at ease*. In addition, I have previous experience of working in hospitality. In my last waitressing job at Ginelli's, many customers became regulars and my employer often *commented on* how well I managed peak periods of the day.

I would like to point out that I particularly enjoy working in busy environments and thrive under pressure. I also enjoy fresh challenges, which is why *I am applying for a position* in your highly-esteemed restaurant.

I hope you will consider my application and look forward to hearing from you in the future. Should you require any further information, *do not hesitate to contact me. I can be reached* on 0798 400200 at any time from 9 a.m. to 6 p.m.

Yours faithfully,

Level 2 Diary features

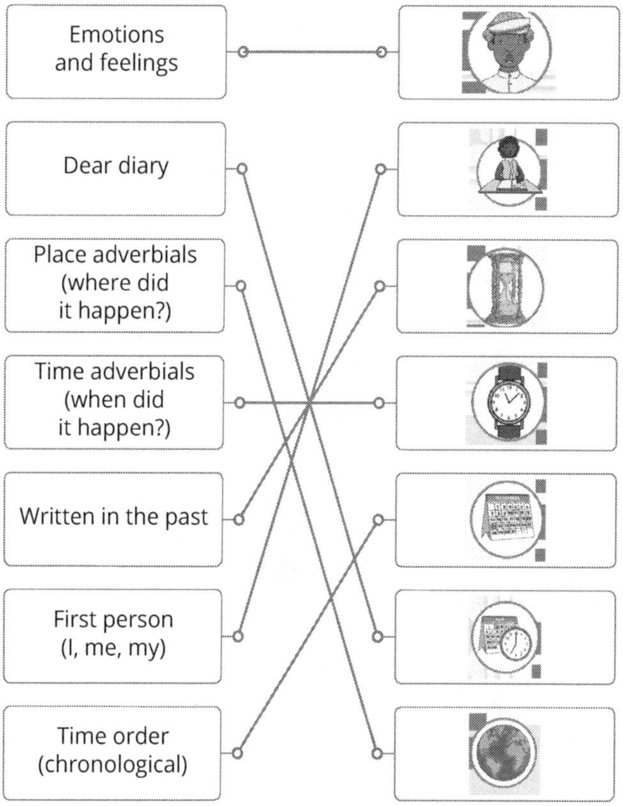

Emotions and feelings
Dear diary
Place adverbials (where did it happen?)
Time adverbials (when did it happen?)
Written in the past
First person (I, me, my)
Time order (chronological)

Level 2 Blog

Name of blog
Title
Personal Information
Subtitle
First person and informal style
exclamative sentence
emotive language
Scarlet Scorch Droppers
home
about
travel
contact
Travel Stories
Around Hong Kong
LET'S CONNECT
SUBSCRIBE VIA EMAIL

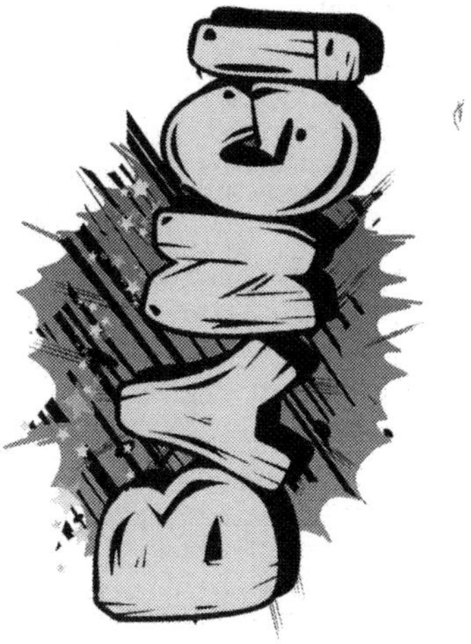

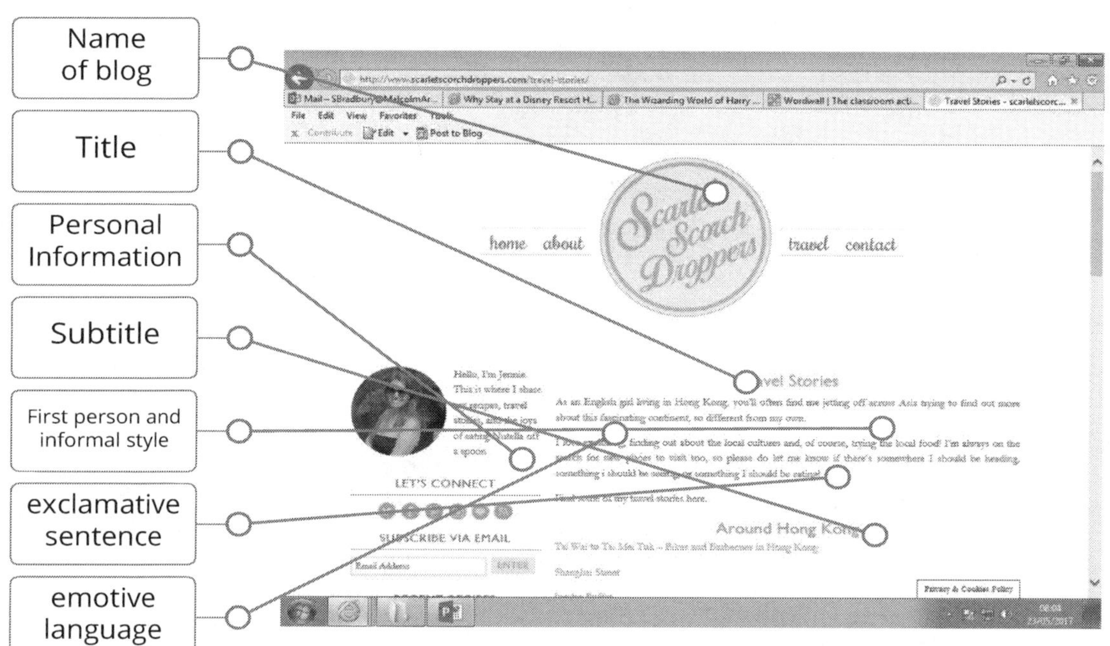

Level 2 Language Features Crossword

Level 2 Language Features Quiz 1

1. I've told you a thousand times!
2. What time do you call this?
3. Reuse, Reduce, Recycle
4. Over the moon
5. Her eyes were like diamonds
6. The world is a stage
7. Your country needs YOU!
8. Peter Piper picked a pepper
9. BANG CRASH WALLOP
10. The vine wrapped its arms around the house
11. 100 percent of people will die

T	R	Z	V	J	E	N	Q	K	J	C	E	H	G	M	W	I	H	Q
R	I	I	P	D	D	X	M	R	V	H	X	O	L	N	W	L	S	Z
H	B	X	K	J	T	V	L	U	T	A	B	H	C	G	T	S	Q	L
E	N	P	I	C	J	Y	N	L	P	Z	X	I	R	K	C	X	R	P
T	A	T	B	X	K	U	Y	E	E	M	E	T	A	P	H	O	R	A
O	G	N	O	C	H	O	D	O	R	X	D	L	E	N	R	M	E	L
R	O	C	W	V	Y	A	U	F	S	J	Z	D	C	K	N	O	S	L
I	N	T	B	M	P	T	E	T	O	O	U	I	B	B	C	T	T	I
C	O	Z	M	U	E	S	I	H	N	T	E	R	C	S	B	G	B	T
A	M	C	P	X	R	J	X	R	I	K	R	E	P	T	Y	U	H	E
L	A	U	G	T	B	H	F	E	F	I	W	C	B	A	N	H	J	R
Q	T	I	M	P	O	U	B	E	I	C	I	T	W	T	S	T	V	A
U	E	K	J	D	L	V	X	Q	C	X	D	A	U	I	B	Q	Y	T
E	O	Q	H	B	E	S	D	F	A	P	I	D	Y	S	I	B	W	I
S	P	K	Q	Z	U	I	D	R	T	L	O	D	T	T	W	C	G	O
T	I	X	E	C	P	M	W	J	I	U	M	R	I	I	S	Z	H	N
I	A	D	D	V	O	I	P	B	O	I	S	E	B	C	L	J	D	Z
O	B	Q	L	R	A	L	H	U	N	K	P	S	W	S	M	F	H	V
N	Y	K	R	A	A	E	G	O	X	W	U	S	N	S	W	Y	X	K

Level 2 Language Features Quiz 2 Jumbled IDIOMS

1. ti 's a eeipc fo cake
it ' s a piece of cake

2. bate ndruoa teh bush
beat around the bush

3. utrhohg ikhtc adn thin
through thick and thin

4. btei het ltbule
bite the bullet

5. it ksate tow to taogn
it takes two to tango

6. go ndwo ni msefal
go down in flames

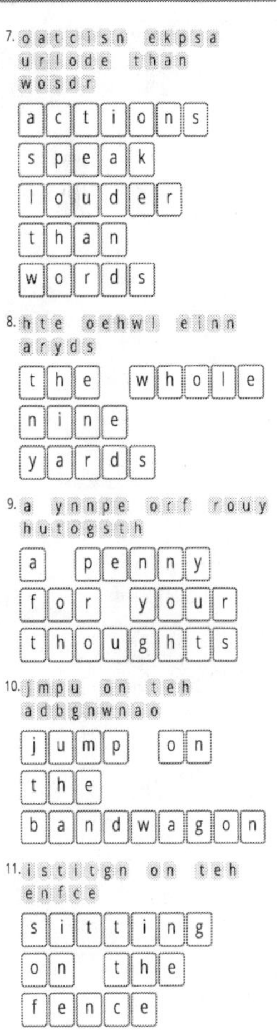

Level 2 Language Features Quiz 3 Rhetorical question or not?

1. What time do you call this?

   A [X] Rhetorical question　　B [ ] Not rhetorical question

2. What did you eat for lunch today?

   A [ ] Rhetorical question　　B [X] Not rhetorical question

3. Going to bed late will leave you feeling tired in the morning. Who knew?

   A [X] Rhetorical question　　B [ ] Not rhetorical question

4. Who is your favourite football player?

   A [ ] Rhetorical question　　B [X] Not rhetorical question

5. Every year, millions of trees are cut down and many animals loose their homes. Would you like it if your home was cut down?

   A [X] Rhetorical question　　B [ ] Not rhetorical question

6. Cheetahs are 3 times faster than the average human. How amazing is that?

   A [X] Rhetorical question　　B [ ] Not rhetorical question

7. What are you doing next weekend?

   A [ ] Rhetorical question　　B [X] Not rhetorical question

8. Isn't life wonderful?

   A [X] Rhetorical question　　B [ ] Not rhetorical question

9. What did you eat for breakfast?

   A [ ] Rhetorical question　　B [X] Not a rhetorical question

Level 2 Language Features Quiz 4 Oxymoron

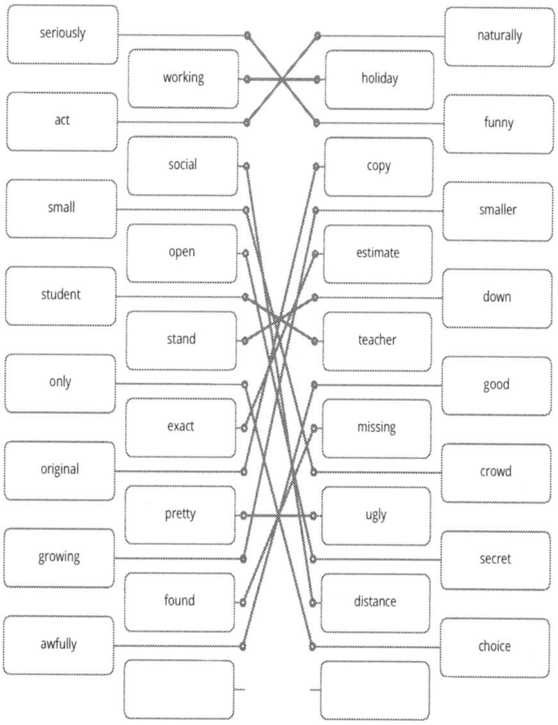

seriously	working	holiday	naturally
act	social	copy	funny
small	open	estimate	smaller
student	stand	teacher	down
only	exact	missing	good
original	pretty	ugly	crowd
growing	found	distance	secret
awfully			choice

Level 2 Language Features Quiz 7

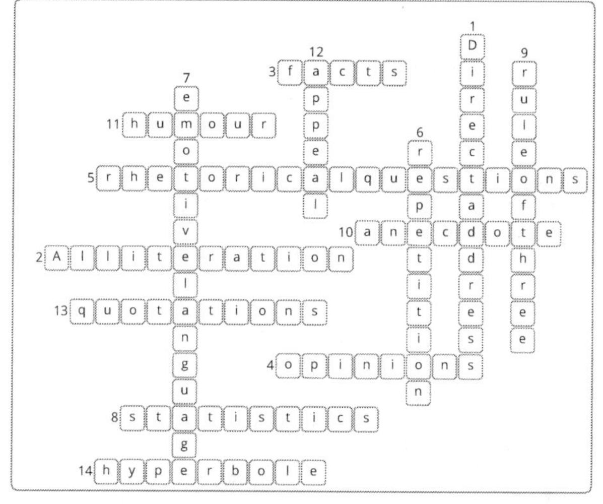

Across

2. repetition of words starting with same letter (12)
3. stating something that's objective (5)
4. stating something that's subjective (8)
5. questions that don't require answer (10,9)
8. using numbers, percentages etc (10)
10. short story to illustrate point (8)
11. making audience laugh or smile (6)
13. reporting wise or respected words (10)
14. exaggerating for effect (9)

Down

1. speaking to the audience "you" (6,7)
6. stating something more than once for effect (10)
7. Language that appeals to emotions (pathos) (7,8)
9. List of three for effect (4,2,5)
12. call for action (6)

Level 2 Language Features Quiz 5 Hyperbole or not......... ????

1. It was so cold, I saw penguins wearing hats!

A [X] Hyperbole

B [ ] Not Hyperbole

2. The film was so bad, I thought I would die of boredom!

A [X] Hyperbole B [ ] Not Hyperbole

3. I like to drink coffee in the morning.

A [ ] Hyperbole B [X] Not Hyperbole

4. It's so hot, you can fry an egg on the pavement.

A [X] Hyperbole B [ ] Not Hyperbole

5. The bus is often late.

A [ ] Hyperbole

B [X] Not Hyperbole

6. I think I've eaten my own body weight in chocolate!

A [X] Hyperbole

B [ ] Not Hyperbole

7. I'm so tired I could sleep for a week.

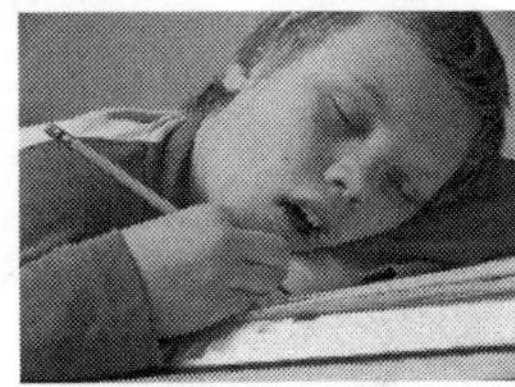

A [X] Hyperbole B [ ] Not Hyperbole

8. He always wears a coat when it's cold.

A [ ] Hyperbole

B [X] Not Hyperbole

9. She ran like the wind.

A [X] Hyperbole B [ ] Not Hyperbole

10. My leg hurts.

A [ ] Hyperbole B [X] Not Hyperbole

Level 2 Language Features Quiz 6 Simile or Metaphor?

Write in the item numbers in the list of boxes for each group

Similes 2 5 6 7 9 11 12 13 14 20

Metaphors 1 3 4 8 10 15 16 17 18 19

1 I'm a night owl.

2 Della is as strong as an ox.

3 Baby, you're a firework.

4 Trouble is a friend of mine.

5 That was as easy as shooting fish in a barrel.

6 My brother and sister fight like cats and dogs.

7 Karen ran like the wind.

8 He rules with an iron fist.

9 That film was like watching paint dry.

10 Let's get all our ducks in a row.

11 Veronica sings like an angel.

12 My room is as clean as a whistle.

13 You're as cold as ice.

14 He is as brave as a lion.

15 Emma was the black sheep of the family.

16 Bob has a heart of gold.

17 It's raining cats and dogs.

18 Dylan is a ray of light.

19 You ain't nothin' but a hound dog.

20 Shelly was as quiet as a mouse.

Level 2 Simile or Metaphor

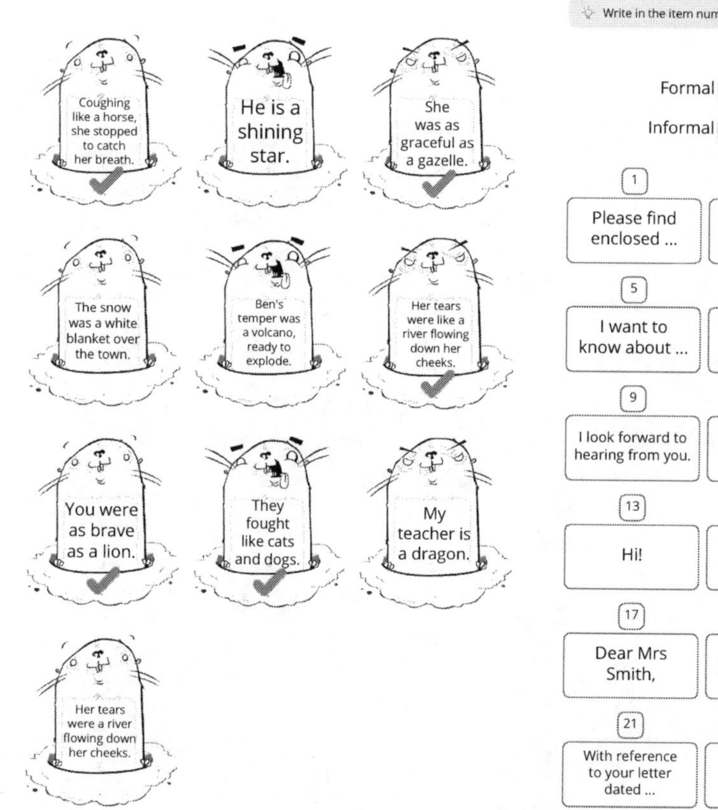

Level 2 Formal and Informal Letters

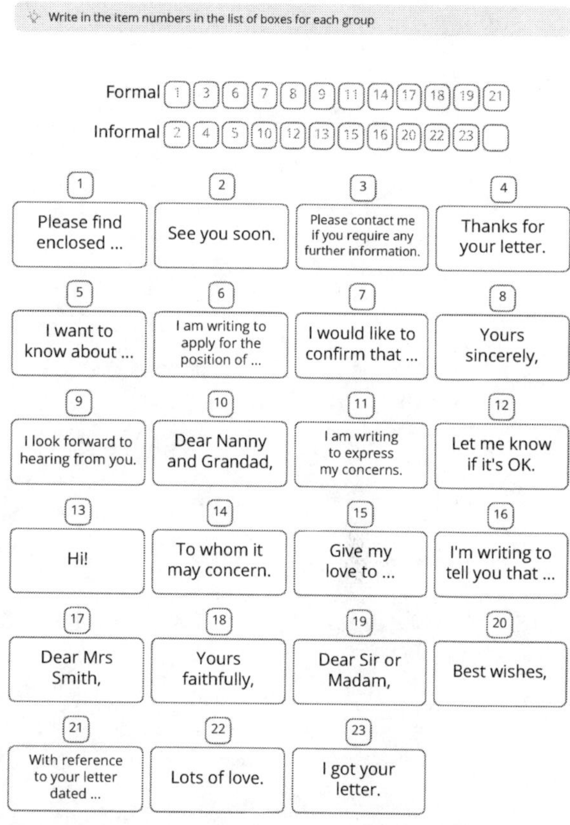

Formal v Informal Level 2 Quiz 3

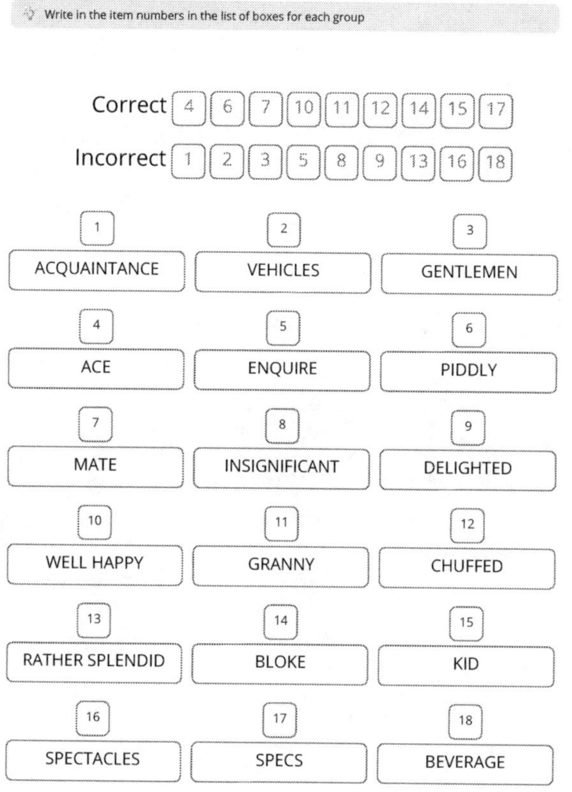

Level 2 Fact or Opinion? Flying

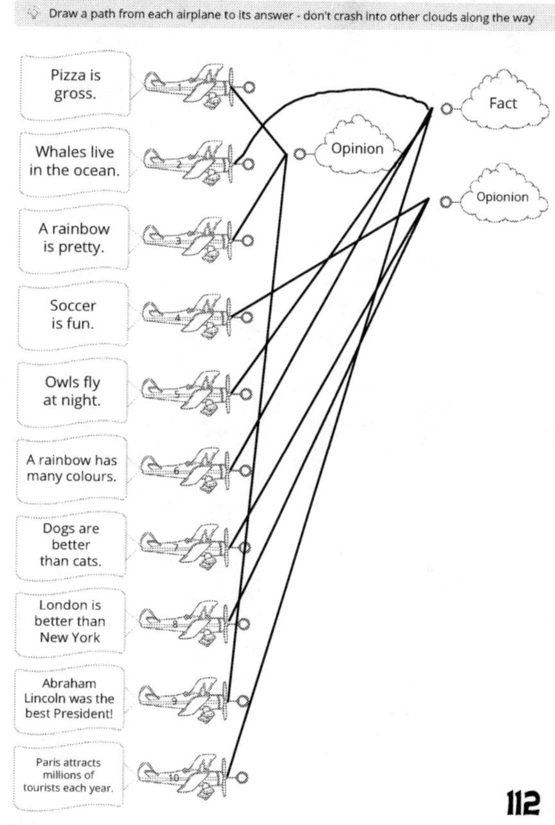

Level 2 Fact or Opinion

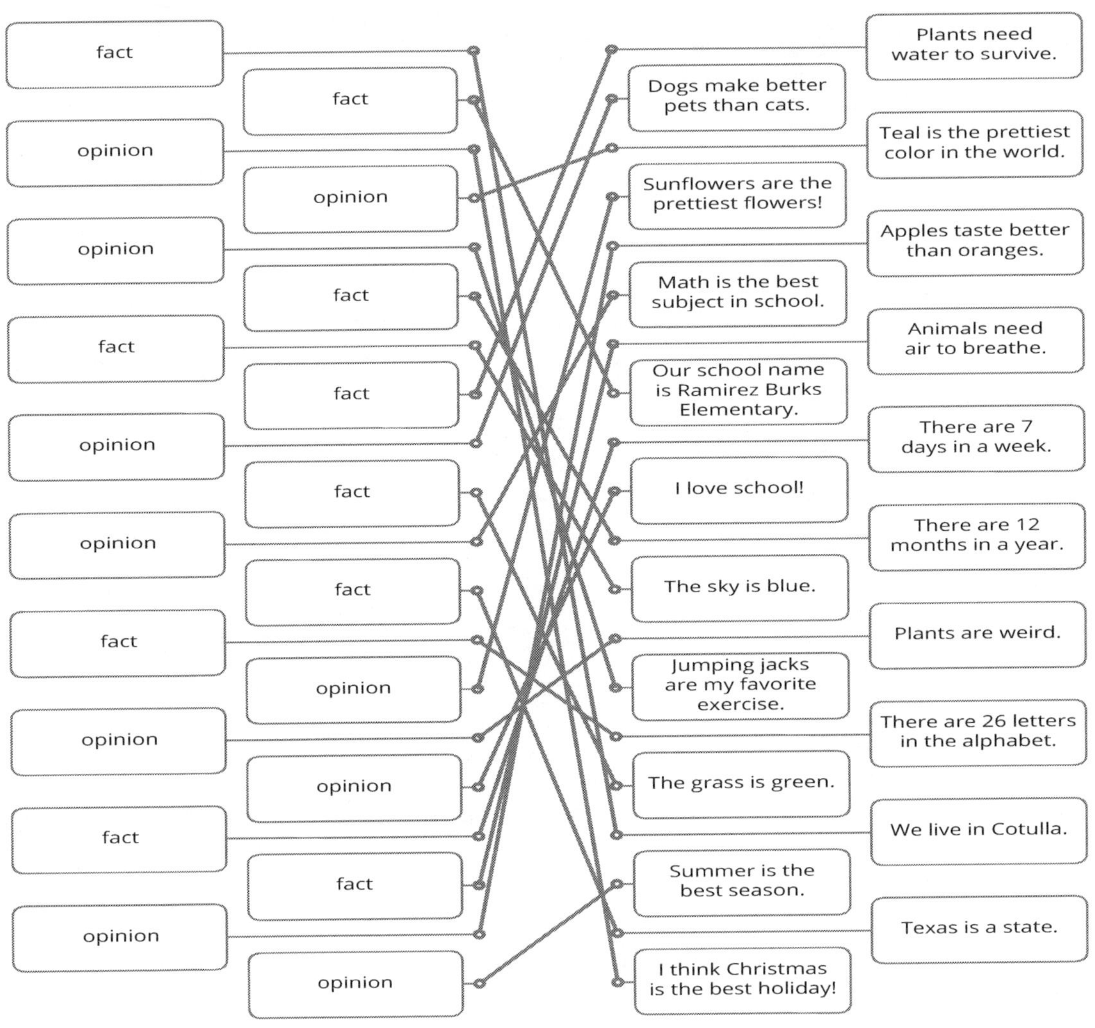

SLANG/Very Informal	INFORMAL/normal	FORMAL
Wanna	Want to	Would like to
Gonna	Going to	Intending to
Y'all	You all	All of you
Dude	Guy/Buddy	Gentleman
Chill	Relax/Hang out	Unwind
Awesome	Cool/Great	Remarkable
Laid-back	Easygoing	Relaxed
Outta	Out of	Outside of
Kinda	Kind of	Somewhat
Bummer	Disappointment	Unfortunate

Level 2 Fact v Opinion Quiz 1

1. The sky is blue (sometimes).
   A [X] fact B [ ] opinion
2. Purple is the prettiest colour in the world.
   A [ ] fact B [X] opinion
3. The grass is green in the Winter.
   A [X] fact B [ ] opinion
4. Apples taste better than oranges.
   A [X] opinion B [ ] fact
5. Dogs make better pets than cats.
   A [ ] fact B [X] opinion
6. California is better than Florida.
   A [X] opinion B [ ] fact
7. London is great.
   A [ ] fact B [X] opinion
8. London is a large city.
   A [X] fact B [ ] opinion
9. Tea is much nicer than coffee.
   A [ ] fact B [X] opinion
10. There are 26 letters in the alphabet.
    A [X] fact B [ ] opinion
11. Summer is the best season.
    A [ ] fact B [X] opinion
12. English is the best subject in college!
    A [X] opinion B [ ] fact
13. The flight from London to New York is shorter than flying from London to Los Angeles.
    A [ ] opinion B [X] fact
14. There are 7 days in a week.
    A [X] fact B [ ] opinion
15. Plants need water to survive.
    A [X] fact B [ ] opinion
16. Sunflowers are the prettiest flowers!
    A [ ] fact B [X] opinion
17. Jumping jacks are the best exercise.
    A [X] opinion B [ ] fact
18. There are 12 months in a year.
    A [ ] opinion B [X] fact
19. Plants are weird.
    A [X] opinion B [ ] fact
20. Animals need air to breathe.
    A [ ] opinion B [X] fact

Level 2 Fact vs Opinion Quiz 2

Write in the item numbers in the list of boxes for each group

Fact: 1, 7, 9, 10, 13, 17, 18, 20, 21, 22, 23, 24, 26

Opinion: 2, 3, 4, 5, 6, 8, 11, 12, 14, 15, 16, 19, 25

1. School uniforms are a great idea
2. Exercise is good for you
3. Toast is better than Crumpets
4. Paris is the capital city of France
5. Monopoly is a board game
6. Monopoly is a great board game
7. Bran Flakes are the perfect breakfast
8. Eating vegetables is good for you
9. You should get a haircut
10. Some farmers in Lincolnshire grow vegetables
11. People in Manchester are friendlier than those in London
12. Charles III is the King of England
13. Kids on computers is never good
14. Some schools make their pupils wear uniforms
15. New York is a city
16. Money brings happiness
17. The Battle of Hastings was in 1066
18. Carrots are better than sprouts
19. Golden Delicious and Granny Smith are apples
20. Eating breakfast is good for you
21. Trainers are more comfortable than shoes
22. All children should play Cricket
23. Cricket is a fantastic sport
24. Parrots are the most intelligent birds
25. Joe Biden was the 46th President of the USA
26. All children should wear school uniforms

Level 2 Speaking and Listening Presentation Quiz 1

Write in the item numbers in the list of boxes for each group

DO this! 2, 5, 8, 3, 7

DON'T do this! 1, 6, 10, 4, 9

1. Look very serious
2. Try to smile
3. Introduce yourself
4. Be interrupted by your phone
5. Say the topic or aim of your presentation
6. Talk quickly - you need to say a lot in a little time
7. Finish by summing up
8. Make eye contact / look at the camera
9. Read aloud from a script
10. Speak quietly

Level 2 How do you spell that? Correct or Incorrect?

1. breathe

   A [X] Correct B [ ] Incorrect

2. appeer

   A [ ] Correct B [X] Incorrect

3. exercise

   A [X] Correct B [ ] Incorrect

4. favorite

   A [X] Correct B [ ] Incorrect

5. bisness

   A [ ] Correct B [X] Incorrect

6. miniture

   A [ ] Correct B [X] Incorrect

7. recommend

   A [X] Correct B [ ] Incorrect

8. eighth

   A [X] Correct B [ ] Incorrect

9. excersize

   A [ ] Correct B [X] Incorrect

10. certun

    A [ ] Correct B [X] Incorrect

11. definate

    A [ ] Correct B [X] Incorrect

12. favourite

    A [ ] Correct B [X] Incorrect

13. separate

    A [X] Correct B [ ] Incorrect

14. breethe

    A [ ] Correct B [X] Incorrect

15. tragedy

    A [X] Correct B [ ] Incorrect

16. build

    A [X] Correct B [ ] Incorrect

17. awkward

    A [X] Correct B [ ] Incorrect

18. aith

    A [ ] Correct B [X] Incorrect

19. breadth

    A [X] Correct B [ ] Incorrect

20. lesure

    A [ ] Correct B [X] Incorrect

21. buetiful

    A [ ] Correct B [X] Incorrect

22. calendar

    A [X] Correct B [ ] Incorrect

23. caught

    A [X] Correct B [ ] Incorrect

24. queue

    A [X] Correct B [ ] Incorrect

25. calander

    A [ ] Correct B [X] Incorrect

26. arkward

    A [ ] Correct B [X] Incorrect

27. believe

    A [X] Correct B [ ] Incorrect

28. beautiful

    A [X] Correct B [ ] Incorrect

Level 2 Spelling Quiz 1

1. s i c l s a b e e c
a c c e s s i b l e

2. n d i a t y c l c l a e
a c c i d e n t a l l y

3. c t i a u n q a
a c q u a i n t

4. i u c a r e q
a c q u i r e

5. a d i e t s m t e n r e v
a d v e r t i s e m e n t

6. n a u l n a
a n n u a l

7. r a p c a a n e e p
a p p e a r a n c e

8. r a n e e n a r m t g
a r r a n g e m e n t

9. a w w a r d k
a w k w a r d

10. u l e i u b t a f
b e a u t i f u l

11. u a e b s e c
b e c a u s e

12. e i e b v e l
b e l i e v e

13. i t e e f b t d e n
b e n e f i t t e d

14. a r d n e a l c
c a l e n d a r

15. o c o e h s
c h o o s e

Level 2 Spelling Whack a Mole

1. accessible 2. accidentally 3. acquaint 4. acquire
5. advertisement 6. annual 7. appearance 8. arrangement
9. awkward 10. beautiful 11. because 12. believe
13. benefitted 14. calendar 15. choose

LEVEL 2 SPELLING QUIZ 2

1. ceiling
2. committee
3. comparative
4. conscience
5. conscientious
6. conscious
7. criticism
8. deceit
9. defense
10. description
11. desirable
12. desparately
13. difference
14. disagreeable
15. disappear

Y	B	T	K	J	M	V	R	C	R	I	T	I	C	I	S	M
L	C	O	M	M	I	T	T	E	E	C	D	D	S	E	E	U
J	F	O	V	W	Z	I	Z	F	W	O	I	I	X	B	D	A
F	C	O	N	S	C	I	O	U	S	N	S	S	I	V	E	H
F	D	E	S	I	R	A	B	L	E	S	A	A	X	V	S	P
Z	H	K	E	O	W	D	M	Z	P	C	P	G	Z	O	P	C
R	U	U	P	K	I	P	N	R	L	I	P	R	J	S	A	O
V	B	C	E	I	L	I	N	G	S	E	E	E	W	V	R	N
A	F	D	T	G	L	Z	D	J	P	N	A	E	A	O	A	S
M	G	S	T	D	V	V	T	P	L	T	R	A	C	X	T	C
D	I	F	F	E	R	E	N	C	E	I	K	B	F	S	E	I
D	J	A	Y	U	M	Y	V	N	U	O	C	L	R	V	L	E
E	Q	W	W	W	N	U	H	E	W	U	S	E	A	F	Y	N
C	Q	J	Q	K	N	A	W	O	C	S	V	V	Q	F	X	C
E	C	O	M	P	A	R	A	T	I	V	E	F	J	G	D	E
I	Q	D	E	F	E	N	S	E	P	A	Q	J	B	R	R	V
T	D	D	E	S	C	R	I	P	T	I	O	N	Y	E	X	B

1. n i e i c l g
c e i l i n g

2. m i o c e t m e t
c o m m i t t e e

3. a t o m e a p v r i c
c o m p a r a t i v e

4. o c e c n i n s e c
c o n s c i e n c e

5. i t c s u c s n n e o i o
c o n s c i e n t i o u s

6. s c o c u i n s o
c o n s c i o u s

7. t i r c s c i m i
c r i t i c i s m

8. d c e t i e
d e c e i t

9. s f e n d e e
d e f e n s e

10. r t e s n p c o i i d
d e s c r i p t i o n

11. i r e d l a s e b
d e s i r a b l e

12. a t e s y a p l r e d
d e s p a r a t e l y

13. i e e c n r f f e d
d i f f e r e n c e

14. g e e r b a i a e d l s
d i s a g r e e a b l e

15. a p i d a p s r e
d i s a p p e a r

LEVEL 2 SPELLING QUIZ 3

1. dissatisfied
2. eighth
3. efficient
4. embarrassment
5. excellent
6. excessive
7. exciting
8. excitement
9. exercise
10. exhilarating
11. existence
12. extraordinary
13. favorite
14. fortunately
15. fortieth

O	R	N	N	C	E	T	V	N	F	O	R	T	I	E	T	H
E	R	J	R	T	F	L	G	O	J	Q	I	Y	V	I	D	I
M	E	E	H	I	F	Z	V	V	W	V	R	D	O	E	E	E
B	X	X	C	A	I	N	V	P	V	R	A	J	I	E	T	X
A	H	C	E	V	C	N	O	I	K	J	G	F	S	T	F	T
R	I	I	X	H	I	Z	R	S	C	N	S	I	O	V	O	R
R	L	T	C	Y	E	J	X	K	I	I	C	K	D	S	R	A
A	A	E	E	P	N	X	O	T	T	R	X	T	M	I	T	O
S	R	M	S	E	T	L	I	A	E	V	G	Z	O	D	U	R
S	A	E	S	F	E	C	S	X	E	Y	M	M	I	M	N	D
M	T	N	I	R	X	S	E	X	U	I	U	P	Z	M	A	I
E	I	T	V	E	I	Z	E	W	J	H	G	O	D	G	T	N
N	N	T	E	D	B	M	R	Q	E	G	W	H	H	D	E	A
T	G	E	X	C	E	L	L	E	N	T	C	C	T	A	L	R
M	B	D	I	W	G	J	U	Y	N	F	N	D	O	H	Y	Y
U	Y	F	A	V	O	R	I	T	E	U	N	K	H	D	S	O
U	X	O	Y	E	U	R	U	E	X	I	S	T	E	N	C	E

1. s s t i d i s a d f e i
d i s s a t i s f i e d

2. e h i h t g
e i g h t h

3. f e i i c n f e t
e f f i c i e n t

4. e t b s a r n r s m m a e
e m b a r r a s s m e n t

5. c e l e l n x e t
e x c e l l e n t

6. c i s e s v x e e
e x c e s s i v e

7. t n c i i e g x
e x c i t i n g

8. i e n t c e t x m e
e x c i t e m e n t

9. c s e i r e e x
e x e r c i s e

10. i a a x e i h l g t n r
e x h i l a r a t i n g

11. i n e s t c x e e
e x i s t e n c e

12. e y t i r o r a d x n r a
e x t r a o r d i n a r y

13. r t v i o f e a
f a v o r i t e

14. t l y r t e n u a f o
f o r t u n a t e l y

15. i t r e t f h o
f o r t i e t h

LEVEL 2 SPELLING QUIZ 4

1. fulfil
2. fulfilled
3. gauge
4. glamorous
5. government
6. harass
7. height
8. heir
9. honorary
10. humor
11. immediately
12. imminent
13. incidentally
14. install

T	G	L	A	M	O	R	O	U	S	W	O	B	W
F	E	G	O	V	E	R	N	M	E	N	T	J	A
I	N	C	I	D	E	N	T	A	L	L	Y	O	S
K	H	D	D	O	W	L	B	F	U	L	F	I	L
F	U	L	F	I	L	L	E	D	C	P	H	P	N
H	E	I	R	N	K	O	O	F	E	R	A	U	U
A	L	M	H	M	H	O	N	O	R	A	R	Y	Q
D	T	W	A	H	U	D	P	Z	Y	S	W	K	X
Q	U	Q	R	S	L	X	X	E	M	R	K	J	M
A	E	G	A	H	E	I	G	H	T	E	V	B	A
P	C	A	S	C	P	S	I	N	S	T	A	L	L
V	H	U	S	K	H	O	H	U	M	O	R	V	H
Y	I	G	I	M	M	E	D	I	A	T	E	L	Y
W	G	E	E	F	I	M	M	I	N	E	N	T	D

1. f u l f i l — fulfil
2. l l i f d e l u f — fulfilled
3. g g e u a — gauge
4. a o o m s u r l g — glamorous
5. n n o e t m g v r e — government
6. a a r h s s — harass
7. g e i h h t — height
8. r i e h — heir
9. o h y r o a r n — honorary
10. o h r m u — humor
11. i d i e e t m l m y a — immediately
12. m i t n i e n m — imminent
13. n i a d c y l l i e t n — incidentally
14. s l i t a l n — install

LEVEL 2 SPELLING QUIZ 5

1. interested
2. irrelevant
3. knowledge
4. liaison
5. leisure
6. loose
7. maintain
8. maintenance
9. marvelous
10. miniature
11. miscellaneous
12. mischievous
13. necessarily
14. neighbor
15. ninth

U	X	B	H	Q	Z	R	M	O	Y	E	B	F	O	E	U
Y	M	S	E	T	K	N	O	W	L	E	D	G	E	F	H
S	A	H	M	I	N	I	A	T	U	R	E	Y	N	R	R
G	R	D	D	E	B	N	E	I	G	H	B	O	R	V	U
F	V	M	K	O	H	J	I	J	I	T	L	X	W	J	F
M	E	I	R	R	E	L	E	V	A	N	T	A	L	D	Y
A	L	E	V	D	N	E	C	E	S	S	A	R	I	L	Y
I	O	W	V	D	R	F	L	I	A	I	S	O	N	V	V
N	U	L	O	O	S	E	Y	E	S	E	N	R	M	Q	X
T	S	E	N	I	N	T	H	X	P	O	T	X	N	C	K
E	O	Q	S	L	E	I	S	U	R	E	Z	S	H	K	A
N	K	R	M	I	S	C	E	L	L	A	N	E	O	U	S
A	C	J	F	Q	I	Y	R	V	L	A	V	Y	P	A	M
N	C	M	I	S	C	H	I	E	V	O	U	S	R	E	B
C	M	G	I	N	T	E	R	E	S	T	E	D	J	I	F
E	E	K	D	M	A	I	N	T	A	I	N	W	L	B	H

1. t r e e s i t e d n — interested
2. r l n e v i a e t r — irrelevant
3. e e n k w o l d g — knowledge
4. s o a i l i n — liaison
5. u r i s l e e — leisure
6. o e o s l — loose
7. i n t a m n i a — maintain
8. a e a t n n n m i c e — maintenance
9. s l a m v r e o u — marvelous
10. e t i m i n a u r — miniature
11. e o s a m s n u l e i c l — miscellaneous
12. i i v h o e c m s u s — mischievous
13. e s r s i a e n c l y — necessarily
14. o g h b n r i e — neighbor
15. n h i t n — ninth

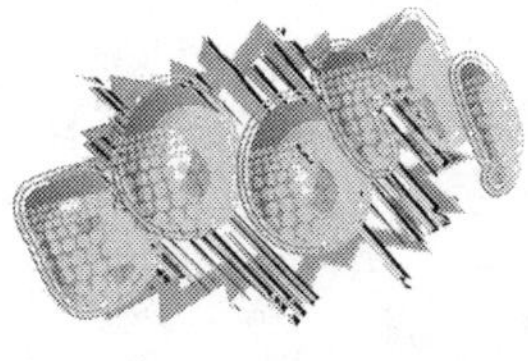

Level 2 Spelling Quiz 6

1. noticeable 2. nuisance 3. occasion 4. occur
5. occurrence 6. occurring 7. omission 8. opportunity
9. panicked 10. parallel 11. parliament 12. particularly
13. pastime 14. playwright 15. possess

F	N	G	P	O	N	O	V	X	Y	F	G	F	C	C	P
Q	U	C	L	C	M	P	L	P	M	S	M	M	F	W	A
W	I	O	V	C	T	P	J	A	T	P	Q	O	Z	J	R
O	S	N	N	U	T	O	L	R	N	L	E	C	D	D	T
C	A	H	P	R	V	R	G	L	O	A	Z	C	P	J	I
C	N	P	S	R	O	T	W	I	C	Y	N	U	Q	Y	C
U	C	A	W	I	M	U	K	A	C	W	O	R	P	T	U
R	E	R	U	N	I	N	N	M	A	R	T	R	O	U	L
P	B	A	M	G	S	I	P	E	S	I	I	E	S	G	A
A	U	L	O	P	S	T	A	N	I	G	C	N	S	E	R
S	D	L	M	Q	I	Y	N	T	O	H	E	C	E	Q	L
T	F	E	O	P	O	R	I	F	N	T	A	E	S	G	Y
I	R	L	N	N	N	M	C	B	H	U	B	W	S	R	J
M	S	Z	I	P	N	R	K	Q	R	C	L	V	Z	C	G
E	A	Y	M	X	P	D	E	C	F	Y	E	U	Z	N	Z
R	L	A	M	X	Y	A	D	H	V	T	E	M	E	X	P

Level 2 Spelling Quiz 7

1. prefer 2. prejudice 3. premises 4. preparation
5. privilege 6. proceed 7. profession 8. prominent
9. publicly 10. pursue 11. quay 12. queue
13. quiet 14. quite 15. receipt

G	M	D	O	N	J	P	U	B	L	I	C	L	Y	A
V	L	P	L	K	Y	G	P	G	R	P	O	P	P	H
E	K	M	Z	L	D	S	G	Y	M	P	Q	W	R	P
Q	P	X	P	E	T	O	Z	T	P	R	U	F	O	E
P	M	U	R	O	U	F	R	Q	U	E	A	X	M	Q
R	T	D	E	X	X	E	R	E	R	J	Y	K	I	U
O	Q	U	P	R	M	Q	D	E	S	U	T	N	N	I
C	U	R	A	P	V	U	F	M	U	D	X	X	E	T
E	I	E	R	R	Z	E	U	I	E	I	U	W	N	E
E	C	C	A	E	E	U	G	C	Z	C	R	L	T	L
D	S	E	T	F	O	E	Q	B	W	E	J	X	B	G
P	U	I	I	E	S	O	P	R	E	M	I	S	E	S
Y	L	P	O	R	Q	U	I	E	T	V	A	E	N	I
G	C	T	N	Z	O	P	R	I	V	I	L	E	G	E
G	P	R	O	F	E	S	S	I	O	N	B	Q	O	P

Level 2 Spelling Quiz 6

1. n t l a i b o e e c
n o t i c e a b l e

2. e s a c n i n u
n u i s a n c e

3. n a s o o c i c
o c c a s i o n

4. u r c o c
o c c u r

5. o c c e u n c r e r
o c c u r r e n c e

6. u c c i r g r n o
o c c u r r i n g

7. n s s o o i i m
o m i s s i o n

8. o y t u o t n p i p r
o p p o r t u n i t y

9. d i c e p n k a
p a n i c k e d

10. l a l e p r l a
p a r a l l e l

11. p r n m l e a a t i
p a r l i a m e n t

12. t l c p y r a u l i a r
p a r t i c u l a r l y

13. i t e a m p s
p a s t i m e

14. p a h i y g l r t w
p l a y w r i g h t

15. e s s o s p s
p o s s e s s

Level 2 Spelling Quiz 7

1. e p r f r e
p r e f e r

2. i d r u j e p c e
p r e j u d i c e

3. s i e e r s m p
p r e m i s e s

4. n i r p p e a t r a o
p r e p a r a t i o n

5. e l r i v e p g i
p r i v i l e g e

6. c d e r e p o
p r o c e e d

7. p o s f r e n s o i
p r o f e s s i o n

8. e n r i m t p n o
p r o m i n e n t

9. y i b l u c l p
p u b l i c l y

10. u p u s e r
p u r s u e

11. y a q u
q u a y

12. u q e e u
q u e u e

13. e q i t u
q u i e t

14. t q i e u
q u i t e

15. e t p e i r c
r e c e i p t

Level 2 Spelling Quiz 8

1. receive
2. recommend
3. relevant
4. schedule
5. scissors
6. seize
7. separate
8. siege
9. skilful
10. stationery
11. stationary
12. strength
13. succeed
14. surprise
15. temporary

X S V J B S K I L F U L V P R
V T J S P S T C S I S Z J W L
O A M T R T E S F I C H N S Q
K T V R E A M U H K I M T U H
K I F E C T P C O U S Y R R J
J O P N E I O C J C S C E P R
C N Y G I O R E S F O S C R E
B A H T V N A E E S R I O I L
N R N H E E R D P C S E M S E
S Y R N E R Y V A H H G M E V
E K Y P O Y I G R E M E E D A
I W P Z Q E Y Q A D N N N X N
Z T N O R P K P T U B M D R T
E F H W K Y S R E L S C Y R E
P B S L K M J T Q E T E M Q K

Level 2 Spelling Quiz 9

1. temporary
2. tendency
3. tragedy
4. twelfth
5. unnecessary
6. unparalleled
7. until
8. vicious
9. vigorous
10. vinegar
11. waist
12. waste
13. wednesday
14. weird
15. wired

G W A I S T R Z E A V S M G U
U N P A R A L L E L E D S H U
D Y D J T C M T Y H Y P A X E
O K T X E U A G L T G Q Z N J
W K N W M N O T V I C I O U S
I F T K P N Z D F X K Y K D X
R P R T O E B P P W A S T E D
E V A W R C T M H G W E I R D
D I G E A E V I G O R O U S J
U N E L R S W E D N E S D A Y
N E D F Y S Q O O S W R V M H
T G Y T K A T E N D E N C Y O
I A H H D R X E D G Y Y D T X
L R S E G Y P I R T Q Y I T P
A L H P C I K M A Z M X F T L

Level 2 Spelling Quiz 8

1. r e e e c i v
r e c e i v e
2. n m r e o d m e c
r e c o m m e n d
3. t e l e r v n a
r e l e v a n t
4. e c h e s d l u
s c h e d u l e
5. s c i s s s r o
s c i s s o r s
6. z e e i s
s e i z e
7. e e p a s r t a
s e p a r a t e
8. g i e e s
s i e g e
9. s l k l i f u
s k i l f u l
10. n e y t a r o t s i
s t a t i o n e r y
11. n a y t a r o t s i
s t a t i o n a r y
12. h t r e s n t g
s t r e n g t h
13. s d u c c e e
s u c c e e d
14. e u r p s r s i
s u r p r i s e
15. r r t a p y o e m
t e m p o r a r y

Level 2 Spelling Quiz 9

1. r m o e r a t y p
t e m p o r a r y
2. n y e e t d c n
t e n d e n c y
3. e t a y r d g
t r a g e d y
4. f t e h w t l
t w e l f t h
5. s r y n s e n a c u e
u n n e c e s s a r y
6. a r e d u p e l l l n a
u n p a r a l l e l e d
7. i l u t n
u n t i l
8. o v c s i u i
v i c i o u s
9. g s i r v o u o
v i g o r o u s
10. g v n r i a e
v i n e g a r
11. s t w i a
w a i s t
12. t e w s a
w a s t e
13. a d e e s d w y n
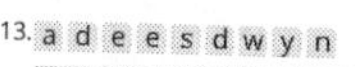
w e d n e s d a y
14. r d w i e
w e i r d
15. e d w r i
w i r e d

Written and compiled by Paul Meade at Media Literacy Consulting, in the United Kingdom. MLC is dedicated to teaching parents and teachers the importance of media literacy in schools and colleges. He and his wife, Michelle recently published Social Media Digital & Phone Addiction - which is available to order at Amazon.co.uk.
Learn more at: www.medialiteracyconsulting.com

Paul has taught English and Writing at Brigham Young University, Idaho, USA and at Boston College and Peterborough College in the UK. He has been a journalist since he was 16 years old and has worked as a news reporter for various television and radio stations both in the UK and USA. Paul has also been an editor and publisher of newspapers and magazines in Canada and the UK for the past 17 years. He currently publishes a newspaper for the exPat community in Canada - which he produces from his home in the UK..

Paul was one of the UK's first Video Journalists - working for Meridian TV in Southampton, and launched the UK's first local terrestrial television station - TV 12 - on the Isle of Wight. As well as publishing his Canadian newspaper, Paul is also currently a Lecturer in English and Journalism in the UK.

Made in United States
Orlando, FL
04 November 2024

53491517R00070